The Hand Book

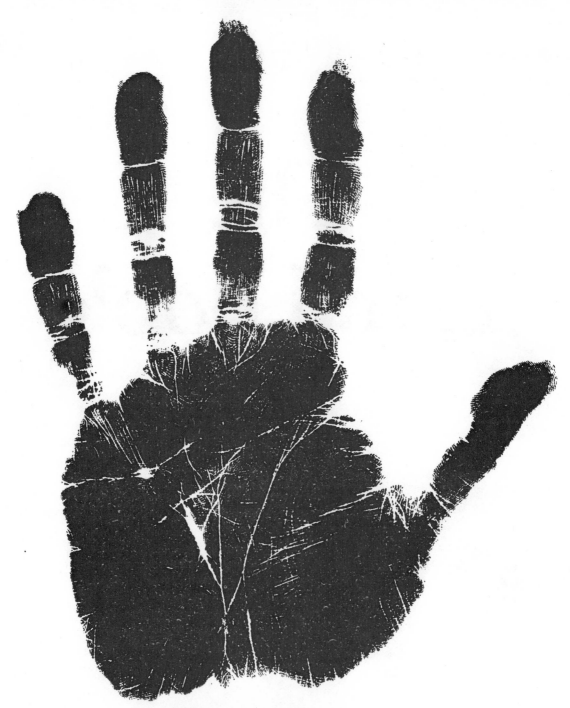

This is the hand of spiritual teacher and author (*Be Here Now*) Ram Dass. Notice how the head line angles down to parallel the life line. The head line also has a section which forks in two, showing that he has a balanced sense of judgment to temper his creative and intuitive leanings.

The
Hand Book

Elizabeth Brenner

Celestial Arts
Berkeley, California

Permission granted for an excerpt from *A Flower Does Not Talk* by Abbot Zenkei Shibayama from the publisher, Charles E. Tuttle Co., Inc., Rutland, Vermont.

Cover design by Linda Harman
Illustrations by Betsy Bruno

Celestial Arts
P.O. Box 7327
Berkeley, CA 94707

First Printing, March 1980
Made in the United States of America

Library of Congress Cataloging in Publication Data

Brenner. Elizabeth, 1954-
    The handbook.

    1. Palmistry.   I. Title.
BF921.B77   133.6   79-5486
ISBN 0-89087-259-7

4   5   6   7   8—88   87   86   85   84   83

Contents

THANKS

To my parents, *Grace and Tom Collins*,
for their unfailing support and encouragement,
To my brother and sister, *David and Rebecca Brenner*,
for being my friends,
To my departed father, *Morris Brenner*,
for many loving memories,
To my first teacher, *Joshu Sasaki Roshi*
for reminding me who I am,
To my first counselor, *Esther Lynn*,
for reminding me about love,
And to the friends who have advised me on the road to health:

    Jas Want Singh Khalsa, M.D.
    Roger C. Hirsh, B.Ac. (UK), C.A.
    Jonathan Krown

May we all keep expanding together.

The section on acupuncture was checked by Roger Hirsh, C.A., and that on psychic healing by Dixie Munroe. I thank them for their suggestions and accept full responsibility for any errors or omissions in the text.

Thank you, Divine Universe, for giving me the gift of life.

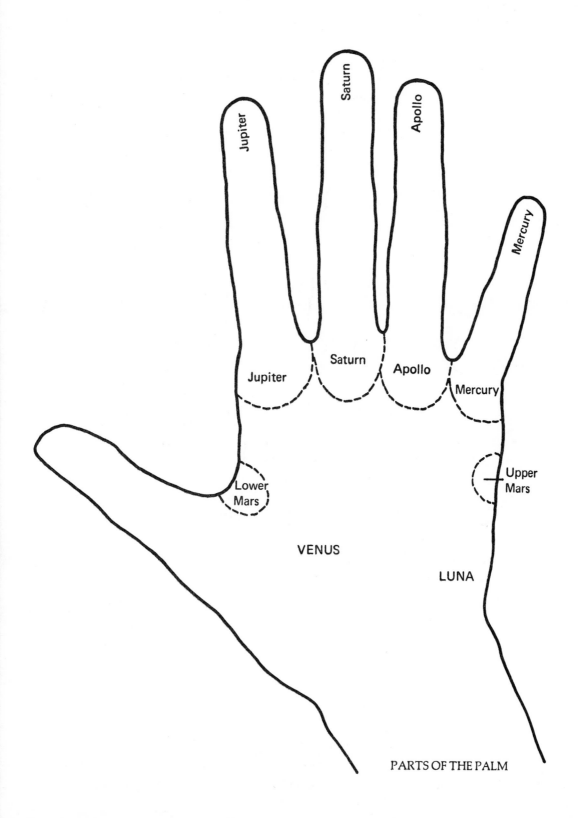

PARTS OF THE PALM

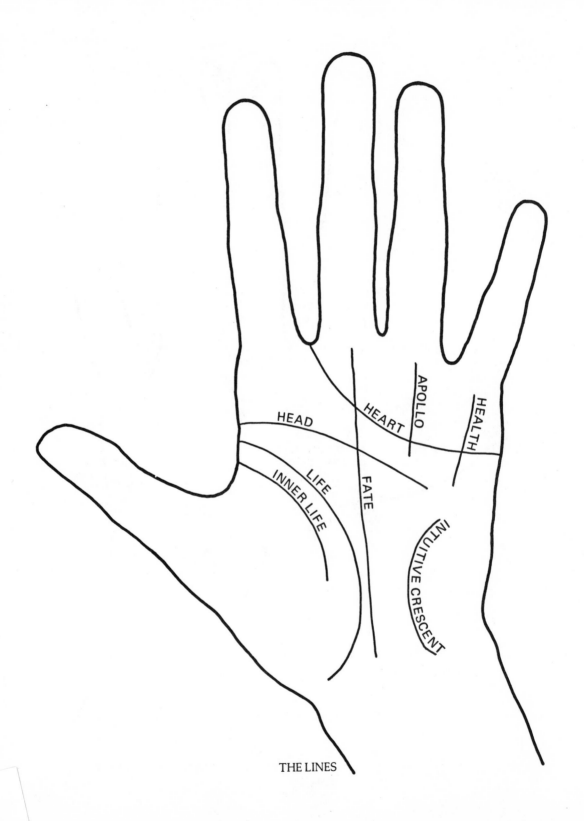

HEAD

HEART

APOLLO

HEALTH

LIFE

INNER LIFE

FATE

INTUITIVE CRESCENT

THE LINES

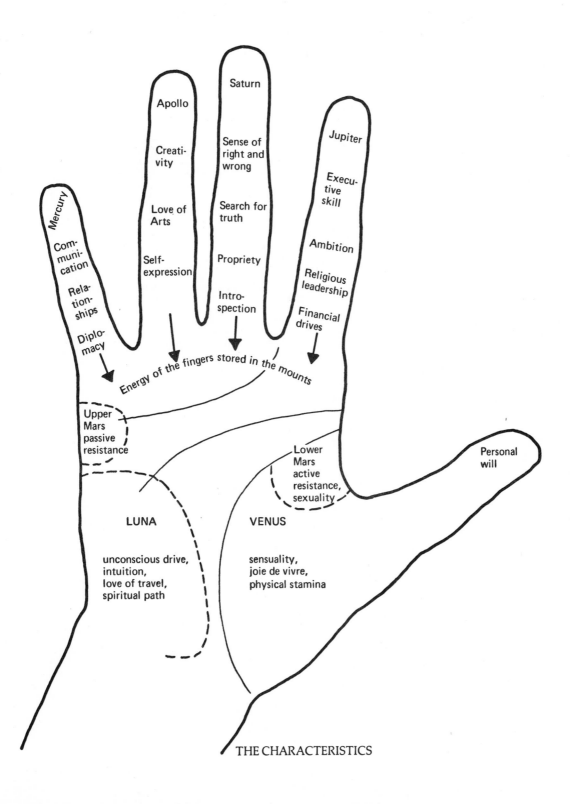

Mercury
Communication
Relationships
Diplomacy

Apollo
Creativity
Love of Arts
Self-expression

Saturn
Sense of right and wrong
Search for truth
Propriety
Introspection

Jupiter
Executive skill
Ambition
Religious leadership
Financial drives

Energy of the fingers stored in the mounts

Upper Mars passive resistance

Lower Mars active resistance, sexuality

Personal will

LUNA

unconscious drive,
intuition,
love of travel,
spiritual path

VENUS

sensuality,
joie de vivre,
physical stamina

THE CHARACTERISTICS

1

The Basics

"May I look at your hand?" A spark of excitement passes between you as your hands meet. He knows he has intrigued you; his hand is nestled in yours and he has your undivided attention. And you are using your intuition and this book to learn more about his character than you could have during a week in a hot tub.

Intuition is natural, not supernatural. You're probably more intuitive than you think; with a little encouragement, the intuition now dormant inside you can be put into action. Reading palms is one way of channeling your intuitive energy. Intuitive palmistry, or interpreting the lines, mounds, and marks on the hand by using your intuition, can be combined with scientific palmistry, which correlates the specific lines, mounds and marks with particular meanings. When you receive information from your intuition as well as your intellect, you will be amazed at how much you learn about the life and personality of your friends (and even your enemies) from their hands. You don't have to be a gypsy to love palmistry.

You are already picking up information from people's hands, forming opinions from a clammy grip or graciously drooping fingers. And you are already using your intuition, whether in sensing something is about to go right or wrong, or feeling someone staring at you behind your back. You probably have more talent for this than you think. As with most skills, people often have more psychic flair than they think they do. Even if you can't demand intuitive flashes exactly when you need them, palmistry has the advantage of being fairly accurate even when your intuition has gone to the Bahamas for the weekend, so you can *always* make a few mind-boggling remarks over the paws of your peers.

In this book, we will simply acknowledge our natural intuition and add some basic tips about how to use that sixth sense to interpret marks on the palm. You will learn which is the life line, the heart line, the head line and all the other minor lines, as well as learning how to interpret the way people gesture with their hands before they know you're looking at them. You will also learn how to generate more intuitive energy within yourself and how to use hand massage to unleash potentials which might be inside you now, waiting to be released. A particular advantage of palm reading over, say, playing Scrabble, is that it allows you to break through social facades with incredible rapidity. I have tried singles bars, computer dating, and introductions by my mother, and this is absolutely the best way to meet people and move into direct communication with them.

Some fantastic stories have come up in my years as a professional palmist. One of the most startling concerns my own mother. Until she was in her late forties, her life line extended about two-thirds of the way down her palm, meaning that she would have little desire to live beyond middle age, and thus might die in her early fifties. I never told her this. At that time she was a widow who, having raised a family on her own, felt that she would have no reason to live after her children were grown. Then she met a man who changed her life. They fell in love like a couple of teenagers. Within four months of meeting him, her life line had extended a full inch down her palm, meaning that she will probably outlive you and me. They are now married and living happily ever after.

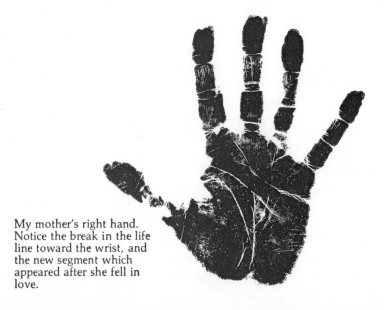

My mother's right hand. Notice the break in the life line toward the wrist, and the new segment which appeared after she fell in love.

Another example is of a well-known poet and singer. His hand shows a pattern associated with creative writers in general. The head line curves down toward Luna, parallel to the life line. Ordinarily, a curved head line is a sign of a strong, creative imagination. However, there are two major differences in the hand of a writer. First, the sharp angle of the line shows an exceptionally powerful imagination which often borders on insanity. (It's a fine line.) Second, the fact that this line parallels the life line shows that the person has harnessed his potential insanity and made it work for him. This artist feels the reading is so accurate that he does not want his name or print published. As he said, "Why spread it around?"

As you continue cultivating your intuition and reading the hands of your friends, you will collect anecdotes like these and the ones that will appear throughout this book.

Using Intuition

Many "sensible" people still are convinced that palmistry is a sham; such people usually have not had their hands read by a skilled palmist. Even though physicists and doctors run headlong into mystery when they try to unveil the origins of life and death, it is a popular belief that the knowledge of scientists is superior to or more real than the knowledge of mystics or psychics. In some cases this is true, but in other cases the "irrational" method is more accurate than the rational. The belief that *all* questions can be answered using only one method of reasoning, such as the deductive method, is as mistaken as the belief that all questions can be answered by one's Mommy. Contemporary palmistry combines the use of intuition with the use of rationally applied principles of deduction. A lot of people will still tell you that palmistry is nonsense, but they are either ignorant or just *afraid*—that you might mention death (as if no one ever dies!) or that you might appraise them too accurately. A certain number of people are simply afraid of the unknown. If they'd learn about it, it wouldn't be unknown anymore, but that doesn't occur to most of them.

The ability to use your intuition is partially a cultivated skill. However, your intuition may need a little nourishment. There are a few basic things to learn about palms, such as the life line, the heart, the head, and the fate lines, the meaning of the fingers, and so forth, but the essence of palm reading lies in opening your eyes to the human being whose hand you hold and using the signs on the hands to reach a sympathetic understanding of the person. Cultivating this basic sympathy will also refine your intuition. You can use it to learn more about yourself while helping your friends learn more about themselves. Plus, being able to read your own hands means you will never again be stuck in a waiting room with nothing to read.

Although you can learn definite meanings for each mark on the hands, accurate palmistry is also a psychic skill. Psychic abilities are based on using intuition. This means that they are based on sensing psychic energy. In this book, "psychic energy" refers to the energy that makes living things alive and keeps the universe humming. It blows through the wind and through your breath; it is that sweet good vibration that dynamizes love.

In everyday speech, "energy" has one significant usage: "I'm full of energy today." Energy here means physical vitality and a sense of well-being. In palmistry and other intuitive arts we carry this notion one step further to mean vitality, or *aliveness* in general. Most languages have a name for this kind of energy. In Japanese it is called *ki*, in Chinese *ch'i*, and in Sanskrit, *prāna*. The concept does not originate from any particular religion or philosophy.

If you don't believe in this universal life energy and in the interrelationship of all beings and events, it won't interfere with your ability to read palms and to tap your intuitive faculties. However, if you sit quietly, breathe deeply, and consider how incredible it is to be alive, it seems sensible to think that we are all somehow tied together. Practicing palmistry has helped me realize my equality with other people. After every palm reading I feel the walls between myself and other people have broken down a little, if only because fundamentally we're all in this life together.

Once you've cultivated your intuition to a certain point, you can look at someone's hand and *see what the problem is*, see the themes of the person's life. If you speak carefully and compassionately, you can address the problem directly without having to ask them what they do for a living. In the same way, if you blurt out everything that comes to mind, you might pull the mental masking tape off someone who has nothing but that holding him together. Would you want some fortune-teller to do that to you? My motto is, soothsay soothingly.

Energy Channels

When water is channeled, it feeds life. When channels clog up, you need to clear them. Like water, energy in human beings runs best in open channels. According to Oriental medicine, there are energy channels running everywhere in the body. When these channels are all open, the person is healthy. Acupuncture treatment is based on the principle of keeping these channels balanced and open.

Now I'm going to stretch an energy channel in your brain and present this:

Lines on the palm reflect the energy channels of the person. They can change as the life changes.

They are like rivers of psychic energy; they grow and change with circum-stance, although their form at a given time indicates the most probable pat-tern the life will follow. If you know how to read energy rivers with insight, you can read hands as accurately as you can read a book.

You can watch the changes in your own hands. Watch the lines in your hands grow stronger and weaker as you feel more vibrant or fatigued, take a look at your heart line after a fight with your lover or boss, or look at the mount of Venus after a good night, and you'll see how the lines and mounds reflect your life.

Discovering and Generating Psychic Energy: Solo and in Couples

Your body is naturally filled with a fantastic feeling of life; this feeling is caused by an abundance of the "energy" mentioned earlier in this chapter. However, lack of exercise, poor eating habits, boredom, and forgetfulness of the beauty of life lead many people to believe that feeling *alive* with full access to natural capacities is something reserved for a small group of en-lightened yogis. This is not so, as you can see for yourself. You are already as full of energy as any guru—you just don't know it yet. To begin remem-bering how much energy you have, try these simple exercises.

Think about the inside of your body. Picture the inner surface of all your skin, the center of your head, and all that machinery inside your chest. As you scan your innards, look particularly at a spot about two inches below your navel, two inches below the surface of your abdomen. A lot of your energy is centered here. If you want to do this more methodically, lie on your back, dressed in loose, comfortable clothing. Take a few deep breaths. Inhale until you feel that the air fills your entire body. Hold the air for a few seconds, then let it all out. Become aware of your feet. Feel them as heavy and relaxed. Picture the warm healthy blood flowing through them. Feel this sensation of heat and relaxation gliding up your legs into your ankles, calves, knees, and thighs, until your entire legs feel heavy and relaxed. Let the warmth move up into your genitals, your abdomen, your chest, then down your arms and up into your head and face. Feel all the cells in your body opening under this warmth like flowers in the sun.

If you have difficulty "finding" a certain area of your body with your in-ner eye, your energy might be blocked in that area. Linger over that section as you scan your body and picture it turning all gold and warm; let it know you love it. Take a few more breaths and slowly get up.

This exercise will help you relax your body and keep your energy chan-nels open. The key to nourishing your energy is *circulation.* The circulation of blood, breath and energy are all related. No matter what you do to keep these three running (it could be anything from meditation to rock climbing), the important thing is to allow some space in your life when your detail-oriented mind can take a break and allow your more basic energies to chime in.

Palmistry and Astrological Signs

If you've ever eavesdropped on two palmists talking shop, you might have heard them glibly drop the names of assorted Greek gods. If a palmist says, "I loved that long Apollo and the full Venus," it doesn't necessarily mean that he's a moonlighting astrologer or classical scholar; palmists use many symbols from mythology and astrology.

Each of the Greek gods was known for his or her peculiar temperament. Venus was the goddess of love and Zeus was the lightning god who had a weakness for heifers. The Greeks also thought that the universe is made of elements—fire, air, earth, water and ether. Not content with this, they divided the sky into twelve sectors, known to us as the Zodiac, and identified each sign as being like fire, air, earth, or water, and as being ruled by a god or goddess and his or her particular attributes. (The Greeks had everything figured out.)

Astrology is based on the relationship between the position of the planets, the signs, and the time and place of a person's birth. Palmistry is a little simpler—since everyone's hands were there when they were born, we don't have to worry about birthplace or time. Palmistry is related to astrology in that most parts of the palm are correlated with one of the astrological houses. Fortunately, we only have five fingers on each hand, so we don't have to learn the whole Zodiac to read palms. Your understanding of the different characters in the hand will increase as the book progresses, but their general attributes are as follows.

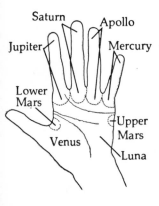

Jupiter   Known to the Greeks as Zeus, Jupiter was the king of the gods, hurling thunderbolts and dispensing justice when he wasn't out having a good time. He represents financial ambition and success, desire for executive power, and in some cases, religious leadership. The thumb represents the person's own will, but the Jupiter finger represents the will of the individual as it is exerted over others.

Saturn   Saturn has the reputation of being a brooding, serious and introspective god with severe and specific ideas of right and wrong. Saturn is actually the Roman name of Cronus, who was Zeus' father. Zeus deposed Cronus and took over the universe, which may explain why the index finger was assigned to him and Saturn is stuck in the middle of the hand. The positive side of Saturn is that he represents the search for truth through scientific or metaphysical investigation.

Apollo   The golden boy of Olympus, Apollo is the god of the sun. He rules the fine arts and creative impulses, and is associated with beauty in all its forms, including music, theater and the graphic arts. In general, Apollo represents an appreciation for aesthetics and a need for self-expression.

Mercury   Little Mercury is the messenger of the gods; he's light on his feet and can talk his way out of any situation. Thus he is known as the god of persuasive speech, successful commerce and diplomacy.

Venus   Venus is the goddess of love, sensuality, *joie de vivre* and sexuality. One of her sons is Cupid; she is also the mother of Eros. You'll hear more on Venus under "Mounts."

Mars   Mars is the Roman god of war. He represents determination, aggression and resistance to obstructions. There are two mounts of Mars, as you'll see in Chapter 3, each of which emphasizes different aspects of Martian energy. One side is the stubborn tenacity of a city holding out under siege; the other is the aggression of an attacking warlord.

Luna   The goddess of the moon, Luna is the patroness of travelers, poets and madmen. The traveling connotation comes to her because she was linked to Hecate, the goddess of the crossroads, before the Roman empire was founded. She also represents the unconscious mind and mystical reflection.

Right and Left and left right left . . .

Always read both hands, but remember that the dominant and the non-dominant hands have different meanings. On a right-handed person the right hand is dominant; on a left-handed person the left is dominant. You've probably guessed that the remaining hand is nondominant.

The dominant hand represents the life the person is living right now, and shows how he is using his innate talents. It shows the patterns of behavior and energy use which he is most likely to continue unless he deliberately tries to change. The nondominant hand represents natural aptitudes, themes and characteristics the person had at birth. The patterns on the nondominant hand also clue you in about the present inner life of the person, since innate tendencies never die. Sometimes they don't even fade away.

Any difference between the hands shows you what the person has done with his innate abilities and what adjustments he has made in his efforts to cope. Be sure to read the differences between the dominant and the nondominant hands, including the differences in tension of the fingers of both hands. Is the Saturn finger stiff on the nondominant hand and flexible on the domi- /

nant? Then the person has a rigid moral code which he keeps to himself while trying to appear liberal and open-minded to the rest of the world.

Comparing the hands is one of the most fascinating aspects of palmistry, because it allows you to watch the ways in which people adapt to the situations into which they are thrown. You see the might-have-beens; you see how people who should have cracked up, judging by their nondominant hands, have pulled their minds together.

For example, if the head line is strong and cuts all the way across the palm, the person has extremely clear insight into himself and his surroundings. It is often quite painful to have such clear insight. Who wants to know? Thus, in many cases the nondominant hand shows this clear-cutting line, and the head line in the dominant hand (that's the one they're manifesting) is curved. This means that rather than continue the endless incision of analytical insight, the person has softened himself by permitting fantasy and imagination to temper his perceptions. Those who might have been bitter social critics or revolutionaries become poets, painters, or visionaries. This allows them to use their insight in some creative form which dulls the impact of seeing reality as it is. If these frantic adapters sink too far into imaginative spheres, which you would see by a head line that lunges into Luna, they risk going insane. All in all, this is a hard kind of person to be. As a palm reader you can help such people understand themselves better, and to realize the compromises they have made. Then it is up to the individual whether and in what ways he wants to change.

Basic Divisions of the Hand

Hand shape and thickness and the form of the lines can vary widely from hand to hand, but there are some basic divisions or zones into which every hand can be divided. Keep these zones in the back of your mind throughout this book and your palm reading career, because they'll help you remember some of the other things you'll have to know. Also, they separate the hand into clearly delineated sectors which you can analyze individually before moving on to the lines, the mounds and the final wrap-up. Palmists use one of two possible division systems—quadrants or the three worlds. We are going to use quadrants.

Look at your hand. Imagine a vertical line running down the center of your (Saturn) middle finger, extending to the center of the base of your palm. The half on the thumb side of this line represents the *outer-directed* parts of your life, the parts which relate to your actions affecting the world outside yourself. The other side reflects your *inner-directed* thoughts and actions. Now imagine a line drawn horizontally across your hand, starting a little above the root of your thumb and cutting across your hand. The area above this imaginary line represents the *active* parts of your life, and the area below it represents the *passive,* or *receptive* parts. You have divided your hand into four sections, which combine into one whole hand in which all the different factors are integrated.

If you look at the illustration on this page, you'll see that the four quadrants are labeled *active-outer, active-inner, passive/receptive-inner,* and *passive/receptive-outer.* Regardless of the shape and texture of the hand, remembering these four areas will help you form a general picture of the person's personality when you first look at the hand. The *active-outer* quadrant includes the top joint of the thumb, which represents strength of will; the (Jupiter) index finger, which represents ambition and the ways a person exerts his will over others; and half of the Saturn finger, as well as the mount of Jupiter. The Saturn finger will be covered in another section, but you can see that in general this segment of the hand reflects several parts of the personality which deal with the active pursuit of one's goals in the world. If this part of the hand strikes you as stronger, that is, if the fingers are longer or thicker and the mounts higher than in the other quadrants, then you know that the active, outer-directed sides of life are exceptionally important to this individual.

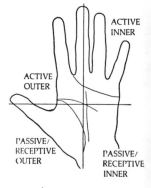

It's possible that no one quadrant will stand out as being dominant. This is a sign that the person has integrated all the aspects of his life equally.

The *active-inner* quadrant includes the rest of our split Saturn, and all of the Apollo and Mercury fingers. All the fingers are essential in the hand's function of grasping and dealing with the world, but Apollo and Mercury play different roles than do Jupiter and Saturn. If you remember the mini-course in Greek mythology a few pages back, you will note that Apollo and Mercury weren't ambitious in the same ways as Jupiter. Apollo was patron of the arts, and artistic creation is an active manifestation of a person's inner experiences. I have also seen very strong active-inner quadrants on the hands of Buddhist monks and professional scholars. While these two groups don't have a lot in common, what they share is a relative disinterest in conventional social and financial success; this is balanced by a strong emphasis on bringing their inner efforts to light through their work.

The other finger in this quadrant is Mercury. Just as the god Mercury had many diverse jobs, so this finger has several different meanings. It relates to the person's way of communicating with his friends and lovers, and is strongly tied to the way he uses words to get what he wants. Thus, both of the fingers in the active-inner area relate to the ways in which a person expresses his inner self to the world at large.

Underneath the *active-inner* quadrant is the *passive/receptive-inner* area, which is made up primarily of the mount of Luna. The lower half of the palm is usually labeled only "passive," but I also call it "receptive" because passivity means more than just waiting to be acted on. It also implies a willingness to receive impressions and be influenced by them. This receptivity is important in the passive-inner quadrant. The mount of Luna is the reservoir of unconscious images and motivations which feed the dreams of poets, mystics and adventure seekers. If any part of the hand is open to subtle messages and intuitive forces, it is this one.

The fourth quadrant is composed of the base of the thumb and the mount of Venus, and is more or less bounded by the life line. It is the *passive/receptive-outer* quadrant. The primal energies of sexuality and physical stamina are rooted in this area; the strength of this quadrant will largely determine the person's capacity to succeed in any physically stressful occupation. If this quadrant is as thick and round as, say, a turkey thigh, the person is very strong and very fond of physical gratification. Don't cross him, in fisticuffs or in love! A less robust passive-outer section does not mean the person is weak; it may be advantageous not to be so physically driven in certain occupations. However, if this area appears to be sucked dry, the individual will have a hard time generating enthusiasm for anything.

The two passive/receptive quadrants are the primary sources of energy for the activities of the rest of the hand. Physical vitality and sensuality rise from the outer-directed (thumb) side and the power of the unconscious mind surges up from the mount of Luna. These combined energies rise from the base of the palm into the "active" half of the hand. Here they are divided and tempered according to the talents of the individual, until finally the energy flows out into the world through the active work done with the fingers; that is, the person generates energy, organizes it, and then does something with it.

I will briefly describe the system known as the "three worlds" because some palmists will tell you that it is valid, and they are mistaken. Traditionally, the hand was divided into three sections: the lower, the middle, and the fingers, which were supposed to correspond neatly with the ancient division of the universe into heaven, earth, and hell, or the underworld. Modern writers have tried to bring this palmar trinity up to date by calling the sections unconscious/instinctual, conscious/social, and mental/intellectual. One psychologist even called them the id, the ego, and the superego, which would probably have made *all* parts of Freud's mind wince.

While one part of the triple world system is valid, it is too rigid to be useful. It is true that the base of the palm, composed of the mounts of Venus and Luna, represents the primal sexual and life energies and is the storehouse of unconscious memories, but the system of three worlds becomes useless after this. It claims that the middle part of the palm informs the palmist of the person's social ambitions and adaptability, but the Jupiter finger is as important an index of social adaptation and ambitions as is the center of the palm. Finger length is significant in determining the type of work—physical, mental, or social—that a person is suited for. If one follows the three-world system strictly, many significant details on the hands will be overlooked.

Even in an art like palmistry in which many factors must be considered before reaching a definite conclusion, the system of three worlds is less likely to be helpful than the system of quadrants, and even that is only a guide around which more careful observations must be made. Whatever valid conclusions you can draw from the three-worlds model are covered within the sections on quadrants, finger length, lines and mounts. All that's left over is superstition which matched the religious views of the period in which it was formulated.

If you can picture vitality rising from the base of the hand and then flowing out to conquer the world through the fingertips and can remember the meaning of the different quadrants, fingers and mounts, you've made a good beginning as a palmist.

Palmistry History

No one knows exactly how old palmistry is. Some sources claim records of palmistry start in China dating from the third century B.C. and others claim that Indian manuscripts predate even this. However, since palm reading was taught orally before it was systematized into written form, it is difficult to say exactly when it began. The fact that few texts survived into the modern era does not necessarily mean there never were any ancient texts, but we have to judge by what's available now. Fred Gettings, a responsible historian of palmistry, reports a few brief mentions of the subject in Aristotle and a passing reference in an ancient religious text. Other than that, there is not much written evidence to go on until the thirteenth century A.D. One thing we can assume is that people have been wondering about the marks on their hands at least as long as they've been wondering about the stars in the sky.

Palmistry in the West is mainly associated with gypsies, but palm-reading systems originated from many groups. Despite the diversity of palm-reading systems, there is, fortunately, a consistency. The three major lines—the life, head, and heart lines—are almost universally recognized. The life line represents basic physical vitality, shows the major events of the life in chronological order, and is the dominant line around which all the others are read. (I'd tell you the others, but I don't want to give away the ending.)

Palmistry as we know it today appears to have originated in India during the pre-Vedic era, and to have drifted into European culture via Greek and Arabic scholars and traders. Although there may have been a continuous oral tradition since the unknown beginnings of the art, our earliest complete tractates begin around the thirteenth century.

At that time there was a vogue for culling Christian symbols from the hand, regardless of the facts of physiology. This trend was aggravated by a penchant for interpreting lurid scenes from freckles and other so-called blemishes. This has become passé. No modern palmist would predict that a person would be burned at the stake as a witch after having been identified by the devil himself. However, the basic meanings and even the names of the fingers and mounts in use today are identical with those used in these old manuscripts. The oldest known palmistry manuscript is the Digby Roll IV, written in Middle English some time before 1440. It mentions the four major lines, the planets, and certain triangles and other special marks.

The history of palmistry parallels that of the rest of Western culture in that it passed through the superstitious realms of the Medieval period into a more empirical approach after the sixteenth century. Although it fell into disrepute toward the end of the Medieval era, when it was associated with witches, vagabonds, and other disreputable characters, our subject was revived during the Elizabethan period. It was more popular on the Continent than in England. A notable figure of this period was an Italian palmist, Barthelmy Cocles. One of the cleverest things he did was to predict the date and manner of his own death. While not everyone would enjoy doing this, his precognitive ability implies that he was an excellent psychic as well as an accurate palmist.

Cocles was also one of the first to use palmistry as a tool in medical diagnosis. There were several other well-known chiromancers in Europe during the Renaissance period. Some of them clung to medieval superstitions about mystical marks and devils while others tried to correlate their observations of the hands with actual life events or psychological traits. One Renaissance palmist, who was also known for his outstanding work in medicine and other intellectual fields, was the renowned physician and alchemist Paracelsus. Although only one of his works on palmistry has been preserved, he made numerous references to the subject in his other works and is known by reputation to have been a reliable palmist.

During the seventeenth and eighteenth centuries, palmists showed an increasing tendency to steer clear of superstition and develop new theories about the nature of man and how the lines on the hand reflect human nature. This increasing rationalism was the trend of the time; from the Renaissance through the Enlightenment periods, scientists and philosophers placed increasing emphasis on the attempt to find rational and empirical explanations for everything. During the period from the sixteenth to the seventeenth centuries the occult science of astrology was outstripped by the more rational science of astronomy, and medicine progressed from being a pastime for butchers and priests into a more careful and hygienic profession. Although the development of palmistry from a popular superstition to a more rational science was hindered by the negative associations with unscrupulous gypsies, rationalization of the basic principles of palmistry led to its being accepted by a few leading intellectuals and scientists of the time.

Writing on palmistry reached an ebb during the eighteenth century, largely because the superstitious writers were too embarrassed to continue the drivel which they'd been churning out for so long, and the newer breed of scientifically-minded intellectuals was reluctant to spend time on a subject which had been so recently associated with these writers. Also, there was much greater interest at that time in discovering how the physical world works than in exploring the inner worlds of psychic phenomena. The only development which would eventually benefit palmists which took place during this fabulous century in the development of Western culture was the growth of an accurate system of physiognomy, or the correlation of certain body types with certain psychological characteristics. This led eventually to the establishment of chirognomy as a reputable discipline. Chirognomy, as you will discover in the next chapter, is the system of classifying various hand shapes and associating them with certain characteristics.

Palmistry per se made a comeback during the 1800s. During this time several great theorists and practitioners, one dashing and accurate popularizer, and one healer/palmist, were all in business. The theorists, on whose work much of twentieth-century palmistry is based, were Adolph Desbarolles, Casimir Stanislas d'Arpentigny, and, near the turn of the twentieth century, William Benham. The dashing popularizer was Count Louis Harmon, also known as Cheiro, and the healer was the Comte de Saint-Germain. Lest you think that all great palmists were men, Napoleon's court palmist was Marie-Anne le Normand.

D'Arpentigny's classification of seven hand types is still used in nearly every text of palmistry. They are: elementary, spatulate, psychic, square, philosophic, conic and mixed. You'll read more about this in Chapter 2. An alternative to this sevenfold distinction has only recently been set forth by Gettings, in his *Book of the Hand.* But more on that in the twentieth century. Desbarolles did not contradict d'Arpentigny, but he elaborated the system of the three worlds of the palm and tied it more closely with occult and Kabalistic symbolism. Although he did not practice rational palmistry, his influence was strong for many years because he founded the English Chirological Society, which produced several books, in addition to a journal called "The Palmist," which were circulated for many years after his death.

Perhaps the most flamboyant palmist of this century was the charming Count Harmon, or Cheiro. Although his palmistic theory is not coherent in the way that Benham's is, he made up for any inconsistencies in his readings with psychic hunches and style. Despite any weaknesses in his written work, he clearly was a magnetic and charismatic fellow who attracted some of the leading figures of his day with his accurate and complete palm readings. His book includes the hand prints of such luminaries as Sarah Bernhardt, Lord Chamberlain, Mark Twain and Dame Nellie Melba. It has been said that Lord Chamberlain left the floor of Parliament for his consultation with the Great Cheiro. Cheiro did all palmists a good turn by helping to make accurate palmistry acceptable at many levels of society.

The above-mentioned Comte de Saint-Germain is only worth noting to suggest the reader not waste money on his book. Although he is reputed to have been a great healer and he may have been a good palmist, the best parts of his works are mostly plagiarisms from previous writers, and a negative and whiny tone permeates every word he writes.

Any respect which might have been wasted on the books of Saint-Germain can be reliably directed to William Benham's meticulous text, *The Laws of Scientific Hand Reading.* His book is complete in nearly every detail, and is coherently presented within a theoretical framework which views the spirit as a sort of substance which permeates the otherwise inanimate body. Regardless of whether you accept his philosophy, his book contains one of the most complete collections of palm prints and photographs of palms ever published. Except for his belief in an intangible life force, Benham approaches palm reading with a hard-nosed rationality that would do any logician proud.

Benham's book bridged the nineteenth and twentieth centuries, and was representative of the new type of palmistry which bases itself on rational deduction and observation. Several modern authors, including Spier, who is a disciple of Jung, and Jaquin, are gradually working to merge the traditional forms of palmistry with current medical and psychological research, which correlates particular marks on the hands with particular physical and mental states. Gettings, from whose historical research much of this section has been drawn, is working on several original theories of palmistry which have yet to be tested.

Each theory and system of palmistry has its own merits. In this book I shall present the system which has proven most useful in my experience as a palm reader. However, there is no substitute for intuitive awareness and practical experience. Remember the basics of palm reading, and permit your intuition to guide you in reading each hand. It would be impossible to catalog every conceivable variation among hands; even if it were possible, such a catalog would divert you from using the compassion and intuition which are the bases of insightful palmistry. Be open to the uniqueness of each hand.

2

The Hands Themselves

Imagine life without your hands. There would be no caressing, no hammering, no pushing, pulling, holding, sewing, throwing, writing, bowling, typing, painting, no learning from the touch of your fingertips and no putting that knowledge into action through your hands. Try to think of a moment in a normal waking day when you are not doing *something* with your hands. If they are not helping you with your work, your nourishment, or your amusement, they are probably involved in some gestures which, deliberately or not, communicate your feelings. If as a species we had no hands with thumbs offset, we would have none of the art, technology, medicine or architecture which give the stamp of creative intelligence to all human works. Our hands—your hands—are miracles of design and coordination. In this chapter we'll learn a little about how they work, how to differentiate between various shapes of hands, and how to interpret the apparently aimless movements of the hands—how to understand what people are telling you even when they think they're not telling you anything.

Physiology of the Hands

Your hands are made up of twenty-seven bones bound together by tendons, ligaments and muscles. Eight pebble-shaped bones make up the wrist. This mosaic of tiny bones is laced together tightly by ligaments and connected to the slightly more mobile metacarpal bones which form the base of the palm. The metacarpals are attached to the carpals, otherwise known as the fingers. This progression from the relative immobility of the lower hand and wrist to the extreme mobility of the fingers creates the mechanical basis of all hand movements. The energy which gathers in the hands is directed and launched through the activity of the fingers.

The muscles of the palm are divided into two main groups, those on the thumb side and those on the little finger side of the hand. There are very few muscles in the center of the palm. This relative flatness combined with the strength of the sides of the hands permits us to wrap our hands around things and grip them. The muscles on the back of the hand extend it and the muscles on the palm flex it. You can see from your own hand that the flexor muscles are much stronger than the extensors; take a small, heavy object which you can pick up and grip easily with the palm side of your hand and try to raise it up and down a few times on the backs of your fingers. A strong man can grip with the force of several hundred pounds, but ask him to extend his hand with a small 250 lb. weight on the back of it and he'll go whining back to the gym. On the feet this muscle situation is reversed and the extensors are stronger, since the feet extend every time we take a step.

Before we explore the nerve supply of the palm, try this experiment: Choose a surface with a very fine texture, such as a delicately woven cloth or a soft feather. Close your eyes and touch the surface with each of your fingertips in turn. Notice any differences in the sensations from each fingertip. Although you are using only one hand, three of the major nerves in your body are feeding you information.

The median, radial and ulnar nerves bring your hands to life. ("Radial" and "ulnar" refer to the two bones of your forearm. The radius is on the thumb side of the arm, and the ulna is on the pinky side. It's easy to remember these with the mnemonic "TRUP": Thumb/Radius, Ulna/Pinky. These words will be used throughout the book, so remember that radial means it's on the thumb side and ulnar means it's on the pinky side: TRUP.) On the back of the hand, the radial and ulnar nerves are most influential, each governing their side. On the palm, however, the median nerve prevails. It innervates the palmar side of the thumb, the index and third fingers, and half of the fourth finger, as well as the areas of the palm underneath those fingers. The radial nerve stimulates the side of the thumb and the ulnar nerve affects the ulnar side of the ring finger and all of the fifth finger. The median nerve is essential because in addition to making the index, third and fourth fingers move, it contains most of the sensory nerve endings that make up the everyday magic of our capacity to feel pain, weight, temperature, texture and the difference between objects. Because the median nerve contains more Paccinian bodies, the cells that transmit sensations of touch, the fingers governed by it are the most sensitive. In your comparative touch test you probably found the thumb, index and third fingers most discriminating. As you recall,

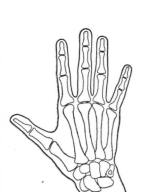

Bony structure of the palm

this area comprises the active outer zone of the hand. It's appropriate that this zone contains our most finely tuned antennae for exploring the outer world.

The musculature, the nerve supply and the mechanical structure of the hand point to the significance of the thumb. The strongest muscles of the hand form its base, the most sensitive nerve in the hand energizes it, and it is in a mechanically perfect position to brace and enhance every action of the fingers. At the beginning of this chapter you imagined life without your hands. Now imagine life with your hands but without your thumbs. True, you could still drum your fingers on a tabletop and pick up things awkwardly, but try to open a bottle, sew, write or paint without them. Many anthropologists maintain that without the offset thumb, even the rest of the hands and our roomy cerebral cortex could not have given us the edge over chimpanzees that we now enjoy.

The thumb is a central part of many widely understood gestures. The Roman emperor's up- or down-turned thumb sealed the fate of many a gladiator. When the thumb meets the index finger it's a sign that all is well. An open hand with thumb extended signifies that the person has nothing to hide and is willing to give of herself. However, when the thumb is hidden inside a closed fist it signals tension, anxiety and unwillingness to face reality. In hand reflexology the thumb represents the head; in palmistry it represents the will. Taking these explanations into account, common gestures take on greater meaning. Hiding the thumbs is equivalent to putting your head in a bag. Twiddling the thumbs is a symbolic embodiment of using mental energy aimlessly. Dr. Charlotte Wolff reports that in interviews with depressed mental patients she frequently observed the thumbs were kept hidden like heads bowed in despair. If a person holds her hands with fingers interlaced and thumbs showing, it is generally understood to show patience and contentment. Interlaced fingers with thumbs hidden are most often seen among people who are extremely upset or depressed. Try sitting with your fingers locked up and your thumbs tucked away—it's depressing!

The Telltale Hands

In addition to the systematized gestures of sign language and colloquial expression, many apparently random gestures tell tales on the gesturer. Your observation of a person's hands should begin the instant they come into sight. Watching your client's hands before she realizes you are watching will give you scads of information, not only about her palmistic traits, but also about how you should approach her in your reading and about her attitudes toward you. A keen observer who looks at posture, facial expression and hand gestures can find out more than she'll ever need to know about a person's health, current emotional state, and background. We'll look at the basic hand postures that give people away, dividing them into those which involve the entire hand and those which involve individual fingers.

Keeping one's hands in one's pockets is more than a sign of bad manners. It shows that the person does not want to reveal anything about herself to the people she's with. If you're about to read her palms, that means you. In his classic text, *The Laws of Scientific Hand Reading*, William Benham writes charmingly about the various postures and personality types a palmist is likely to encounter. Try nonchalantly to observe these postures before the person realizes you're looking or she may change her pose for your benefit. Benham points out, in addition to the secretive hands-in-pockets attitude, the cautious, trustworthy type holds her hands partially open at her sides. As long as the hands seem flexible and full of life, she's reliable and good at business. If the hands are left loosely at the sides and appear flaccid and dull, odds are the person is also flaccid and dull. Benham says this type has a "mind like a sieve." Don't quote him to your friend with the flaccid hands.

Whenever you see an elbow or wrist bent at a 90-degree angle you'll know you're in for a tough reading. The prissy types who hold their hands in this affected manner are usually very self-occupied. Be on guard against people who habitually rub their hands together in a handwashing gesture; they are insincere and love to gloat over their own power.

If the hands are clasped calmly in front of the body, the person is remarkably even tempered and calm; try to match her mood. If the hands are clasped behind the back, the individual has either been watching too many film clips of Prince Charles or is trying to assess the situation carefully before showing her hand. Once she realizes you're not a witch she'll be quite friendly. When the hands are held in front of the body in a slightly defensive posture, like a martial artist preparing for action, the person is calm but also alert and defensive. A small percentage of people suffer from involuntary tremors of the hands; these should be understood as medical problems.

Getting a Feel For the Hands

Remember the exercises in Chapter 1 which dealt with finding your strongest energy center? Review them now because those exercises, or shortened forms of them, will be used at every step in the palm-reading process. Before you get a feel for your palm or anyone else's, wash out your mind. Pause and feel that energy center in your abdomen, chest or forehead. Let your mind rest there for a moment before you even consider receiving information from the hand. This is like setting a scale back to zero before weighing something new, and insures that you will only pick up what the individual hand is telling you rather than what you're telling it. Cultivate a feeling of love for the person who is trusting you to look into her hands. When you've zeroed your psychic scale and felt that little surge of affection, ask the person to hold out her hands in a natural, comfortable position.

At first, just scan that hand. Note whatever patterns strike you first and then keep on looking. Which lines are the deepest? The weakest? Are the mounts full or flat? Which are the most prominent? Is the skin smooth or flaky? Damp or dry? Pale, red or mottled? If the skin doesn't seem healthy, ask your intuition what kind of poison is causing the problem. If nothing comes to you, keep on looking. The answer will come to you later. Also look at the spaces between the fingers and whether these spaces are determined by the natural set of the fingers or by tension. You can learn a lot about a person's lifestyle by looking at her hands, even if you don't know anything about palmistry. Various sports leave callouses, but that does not mean the person is callous. Constant gardening and other physical work toughens the skin, but you should still be able to tell the difference between naturally fine skin toughened by work and naturally coarse skin. Note these signs as possible indicators of the person's habits, but don't give them too much importance. People are often not what they seem. After you've gotten a strong general impression of the ways in which the energy is distributed through the palm, take a close look at the fingers.

In Chapter 1 you were introduced to the Greek and Roman gods who've had fingers named after them: Jupiter, Apollo, Saturn and Mercury. Each god has his idiosyncrasies and each is correlated with a finger.

Jupiter rules the index finger. Since Jupiter was the king of the gods and was also a sort of religious leader, the index finger represents executive ability, financial ambition, confidence in exerting one's will over the wills of others, and in certain cases, religious leadership. The index finger is normally a little shorter than the middle finger and roughly the same length as the fourth finger. If it is longer, the person tends to be egotistical; if shorter, then she lacks confidence in herself.

Saturn rules the middle finger. This long finger mediates between the inner- and outer-oriented sides of the hand. Saturn was a judge and arbitrator, so this finger represents a person's ideas of propriety and of right and wrong. A long Saturn finger indicates a love of introspection and a stubborn curiosity about insoluble questions of existence. If the Saturn finger is longish and slightly bent toward Jupiter, this person loves to be on her own. She can amuse herself peacefully with reading, music and thought. A short Saturn finger indicates that the person has trouble distinguishing between right and wrong. Hang on to your wallet, but remember that this is an inborn limitation which the person may be trying hard to overcome.

Apollo rules the fourth, or ring finger. He was the god of the sun, and patron of medicine and the creative arts. As this is the first finger on the

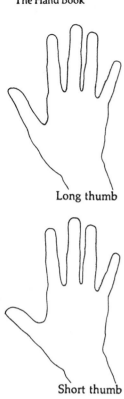

Long thumb

Short thumb

Low-set thumb

High-set thumb

inner-directed side of the hand, it is associated with *expression* of the person's inner feelings to the outer world. An Apollo finger as long as, or slightly longer than the Jupiter finger indicates that self-expression is more important to this person than ambition or money. A shorter Apollo doesn't necessarily mean that art or self-expression are unimportant to the individual, but it does tell you that everything the person does must have some effect in the material world. Remember to look at *relative* finger length—on a long-fingered hand a long Apollo is just one more long finger.

Mercury rules the fifth finger. Mercury was patron of thieves, merchants and diplomats. The Mercury finger influences a wide variety of characteristics, ranging from effectiveness in relationships and sexuality to diplomatic speech. All of Mercury's traits involve *communication.* Someone with an extremely short Mercury finger will have constant trouble communicating her ideas to others, and will frequently consider herself to be misunderstood. Conversely, a very long Mercury finger indicates a special ability for smoothing difficulties with aptly chosen words. If someone habitually holds the Mercury finger wide apart from all the others, she is alienated from her own heart and therefore from the hearts of others. If Mercury is held a slight distance from Apollo it simply means that the person speaks her mind freely.

The *thumb* was never assigned to a god because it is so purely human. It represents the personal will. Indian palmists don't look at the hand or the lines—their entire system of palmistry is based on examination of the thumb. In every reading, and especially if you have little time to read or are spying on someone's hands without telling her, look first at the thumb. Its shape will tell you about the person's basic character, how she makes decisions and how firmly she can carry out her plans. The posture in which she holds it will tell you her mood and general attitude toward life. Reading the thumbnail for signs of health will give you an immediate overview of the person's general state of health. The size and setting of the thumb are also significant. Tradition has it that great men are marked by the great size of their thumbs. Voltaire and Newton are often cited as examples of geniuses who were renowned for their enormous thumbs. However, Charlotte Wolff has done a study of the thumb length of "high achievers" and has found that most great men had normal-length thumbs. Nevertheless, someone with a long thumb is more likely to make something of herself than someone with a stilted, deformed thumb. A thumb that ends near the base of the index finger is short; one that extends beyond the middle joint of the index finger is long.

Before you proclaim a thumb as long or short, note where it is set into the hand. A long thumb set low in the hand is not a short thumb. If the thumb looks submerged in the hand the person is overcautious, absorbed in the passive energies of her life. If it's a little higher than that but still lower than normal, then the person is drawing on more Venusian energy than usual, so she's warmhearted and happy to do favors whenever she can. Gettings

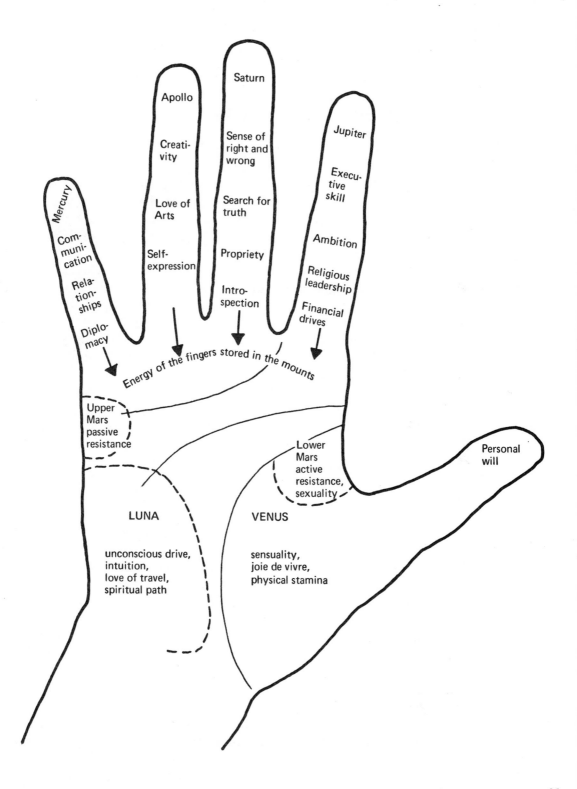

Saturn
Sense of right and wrong
Search for truth
Propriety
Introspection

Apollo
Creativity
Love of Arts
Self-expression

Jupiter
Executive skill
Ambition
Religious leadership
Financial drives

Mercury
Communication
Relationships
Diplomacy

Energy of the fingers stored in the mounts

Upper Mars passive resistance

Lower Mars active resistance, sexuality

Personal will

LUNA
unconscious drive, intuition, love of travel, spiritual path

VENUS
sensuality, joie de vivre, physical stamina

21

"Murderer's" thumb

Waisted thumb

Spatulate thumb

Thumbtip flat, when viewed from side

claims that a high-set thumb signifies a dynamic, outward-looking personality. However, monkeys and idiots also have high thumbs. On a so-so hand, the high thumb can show stubbornness and arrogance. On a strong hand, it means great personal strength. On a monkey's hand it means he's perfectly normal.

The thumb is based in the mount of Venus. With this powerhouse as a foundation, it's no wonder it has so much influence. Its two upper joints show how that Venusian energy is modulated as it moves into action. The middle joint shows reasoning ability, and the top joint shows willpower and decisiveness. Ideally, the top joint should be slightly shorter than the middle joint and the whole thumb should extend to the middle of the lower joint of the index finger. The thumb should be supple but show a little resistance when you try to bend it backward. If you can push it over with no effort, then the person is too easily swayed by other people's wishes. If it's rigid and tense, the person is very opinionated and adapts poorly to change. You can't test your own thumb and finger tension because your hands are too closely related. However, it's easy for someone else to test them for you.

Square, spatulate, and conical thumbtips have the same basic significance as square (practical), spatulate (active), and conical (sensitive) fingertips, except that the thumbtip is more significant since it characterizes the person's will and general health. A few thumbtip shapes do not appear as fingertip shapes. A broad, flat thumb shows a firm, careful disposition. This is often called the "murderer's thumb" but it is an inherited trait. With an excessive Venus mount and a shattered heart line, the firmness of will could turn into cruelty, but most people with murderer's thumbs wouldn't hurt a fly. A paddle-shaped thumb is a sign of extreme determination. Do not get in this one's way. A thumb which is conical at the top and has a narrow second phalange (the so-called "waisted thumb") is a mark of a tactful, pleasant personality. If the thumbtip is flat when viewed from the side, then the person is nervous and has problems implementing her wishes, regardless of the shape of the tip.

The way the person holds her thumb is also quite telling. Remember that the thumb represents the will, so its posture is a symbol of the person's overall mental state. Newborn babies keep their thumbs curled up in their fists for the first few weeks of life. It's a sign that the child is accepting her transition into the outside world when the thumb emerges from the little fist and begins to help her grab the things she wants. When a child or adult returns the thumb to its hiding place in the fist, it's a sign that some anxiety or despair is becoming too much to handle; she is retreating. If the hands are clenched with thumbs inside, it's a sign of powerful tension and anxiety. If they are folded with the thumbs inside, read grief and black despair. On the contrary, if the thumb is held at an angle from the hand, the person has a spunky spirit and is happy to face the conflicts of worldly life.

Hot Tips

The fingers are composed of three sections, or phalanges. The relative size of each phalange gives you a sense of the person's priorities: If the one closest to the palm (the basal phalange) is longer and thicker, then physical and sensual pleasures take first place. If the middle section is longer and thicker, then the business world and practicality have the strongest lure. If the top section is elongated, then the person is highly mental or intellectual. The shape of the fingertips shows how the energy is channeled. More pointed tips allow free flow of energy into and out of the hands. Blunter tips slow down the energy passage.

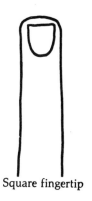

Square fingertip

Fingertips come in four basic types: square, conical, spatulate and pointed. These are general categories, so you can expect to find nuances of shape which cannot be easily classified. The strongest tendencies of the tip shape are the strongest tendencies of the person. For example, if most of the fingers seem conical but have a slight flair at the end, then they are conical/spatulate; this means their sensitivity (shown by the conic tips) will be somewhat energized by a flair for activity (shown by the influence of the spatulate tips). It's rare for a person to have only one shape of fingertips on all the fingers; the proportion of one type to another informs you about the balance of tendencies in the person's temperament.

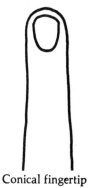

Conical fingertip

Square fingertips signify practicality, usefulness, balanced thought, and a capacity for rational, decisive action. People with mostly square tips are sensible, good at business and can cope.

Conical tips (slightly narrower at the top than at the base) indicate the same thing as conical hands—sensitivity, love of the arts, receptivity to outside stimuli, impulsiveness, accurate intuition, and quick-mindedness without intellectuality.

Spatulate tips are flared at the top. They indicate a creative flair for action, an impulsive and adventurous spirit, and an ability to instinctively arrange things and people into new and interesting arrangements. If a spatulate-tipped person is stuck in a situation which limits her creativity and mobility, she is a miserable spatula indeed.

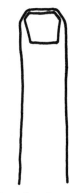

Spatulate fingertip

Pointed tips are the most idealistic and sensitive of all. They make excellent funnels for energy entering and leaving the body, which means their owners are often overcome by outside influences which their square-tipped friends would never perceive. Spiritual mediums often have pointed tips, but not everyone with pointy fingers is a medium. More likely, they're too idealistic for life in the everyday world and constantly feel overwhelmed by the nastiness of it all. They are lovely, frail people with a passion for art and religion.

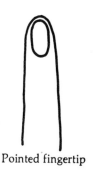

Pointed fingertip

You can see the contradiction between the shape of the palm (squarish) and the fingertip (pointed) in this woman's hand. Notice that the thumbtip looks strong and well-formed; this will help her balance the conflicting demands of her temperament.

The shapes are more harmonious in this woman's hand; the palm is squarish and so are the fingertips. She is stable and practical. Also notice the Mystic Triangle resting between her head and heart lines. In this student of Zen Buddhism, spirituality and practicality are well combined.

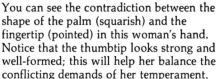

If the fifth finger is long and pointed, it's a sign of potential schizophrenia.

These are the meanings of the tip types out of the context of an individual hand. In practice it's best to bear in mind the type of hand on which the fingertips appear. The happiest people are those in whom the shape of the hand, the shape of the tips, and the overall configuration of the lines are all of the same or complementary types. For example, a square palm with mostly square tips nearly guarantees a stable and productive life, since there will be no paralyzing inner conflicts. A square palm with pointed fingertips would indicate that the person has an innate and powerful conflict between a sensible temperament and a tendency to artsy idealism. Her practical efforts will never be lofty enough for her idealistic side and this attraction to art and mysticism will never seem worthwhile to her sensible side. Spatulate fingertips on a long, narrow palm would produce a similar conflict—the person would want to be active but would lack the energy to fulfill her fantasies. However, spatulate fingertips on a square palm would be an excellent combination. The square palm would provide a solid grounding in practicality and the spatulate tips would add creative zest to all the sensible plans. As with every other aspect of palm reading, fingertips should be interpreted *in context*.

Reading the Fingers, or Family Life on Olympus

Once again, begin with the general scan. Are any of the fingers curved in toward the hand? Bend each one gently back and forth and feel for the tension in each finger. Do they naturally bend away from the palm? How are they spaced, close together or loosely apart? Or are they just spaced out? If there are any marked lumps, ask if the person has ever injured that finger; it is very embarrassing to spend ten minutes interpreting an ice-skating injury. Look at the relative proportion of the three joints. Are any of the joints thicker or more constricted than the others? That is, is the bottom part of the finger chubby or is it wizened in comparison to the other parts of the finger? If it's thinner, then the person is cutting off the energy of the part of her personality associated with that finger. Are either of the joints knotted? The upper knot is the philosophical knot. If this joint is gnarled and thick, it signifies—you guessed it—a philosophical disposition. The second knot is the material or worldly knot, indicating a practical nature.

Remember that Jupiter means personal will exerted over others and financial ambition; Saturn means responsibility and reflection; Apollo means creativity and the fine arts; and Mercury means skill with communication. Ideally, each god should rule his own domain and should not usurp power from his neighbors. When you ask the person to hold her hands out, look at the relationships between the fingers. Is Mercury huddled under Apollo, or Saturn partly covering Apollo? Is Jupiter partly covering Saturn or is Saturn partly covering Jupiter? These unconscious patterns of tension reveal an enormous amount about the person's inner conflicts. Bearing in mind the meaning of each finger, you can interpret the finger language. If Jupiter is covering Saturn, then the person's financial ambition is stifling her moral precepts. If Saturn is covering Apollo, then the sense of propriety and responsibility is squelching the person's artistic ambitions. The tension patterns in each hand are unique but if you remember the meaning of each part of the hand you can put together a character study of the greatest accuracy.

As you bend each finger, sense its tension and flexibility. Does the person leap pathetically to accommodate you, bending the finger further than you intended? Is the finger rigid? Or, most interesting of all, are some of the fingers supple and flexible and others rigid? Ideally, the fingers should be flexible but not flaccid, strong but not tensed. Tense fingers signify blocked energy; supple fingers mean sturdy and flexible energy channels. Bending each finger slowly is also a way of establishing physical contact with your subject. As you listen for the message of each finger, keep your breath slow and your mind open and loving. There's no need to speak at this point in the reading, and the slow, gentle contact of your hands will help her relax.

If the fingers are too soft and bending, the person gives in too easily to others' demands even when those demands are unreasonable. If all the fingers are rigid and flexed away from the palm, the person is probably rigid and unbending. However, some people think palmists like rigid fingers because they're easier to "see", so they tense up the fingers as soon as you start to look. If you suspect this, keep on bending the fingers back and forth until the person becomes bored or distracted and relaxes into her natural pattern.

If some of the fingers are rigid and others are not, then the energy channels in the tense fingers are blocked and the talents associated with that finger are repressed. And you know what happens to people who are repressed: nothing. For example, if a person has conical fingertips and a long line of Apollo, you know that she'd like to be an artist. But if the Apollo finger is curled and the lower joints are dried up, she is blocking her own expressiveness. Suggest she massage that finger until it is as supple and straight as possible and consider taking a class in something she would enjoy. Another common case of "tensed finger" occurs among people who think they are very, very liberal. If the Saturn finger of the *nondominant* hand is tense, then the person's inner moral code is stronger than she lets on. She grins tolerantly at sacrilege but she's inwardly quivering with moral outrage. These people frequently have problems in their relationships because they judge their friends so harshly without showing it.

If Mercury is so tense that the person can hardly talk, if Jupiter is so rigid that the person can't fulfill her ambitions, if all the fingers are out of balance, what would you suggest? Massage is helpful, especially if done often by friends. Releasing the physical tension in the hands has a feedback effect on the mind. When the Apollo finger is limber and relaxed, the individual will be better able to express whatever artistic talents she has. This applies to every possible energy blockage on the hands: Release the tension and the person's life will naturally begin to change.

However, before you spout off helpful advice, remember that some people love their repressions. They have established a workable equilibrium with all their problems intact, and regardless of what they tell you, they might not really want to change. Low-key advice is the most likely to be followed, so preface your suggestions with a disclaimer like, *"If you want to change, you might consider massage, or meditation, or jogging, or whatever."* It's important to respect each person's right to choose the energy level at which she wants to exist. The most helpful thing you can do is to *draw attention to the energy blockage and affirm the person's ability to open up.*

Having identified their relative tensions, we're ready to tackle the way the fingers are held. Listen carefully to your intuition here, because similar patterns can be interpreted quite differently. So take a deep breath and listen to the song that hand is singing! Separation is often healthy, but divorce is unfortunate, particularly when it happens within one person. If any finger is really splay, jutting out vertically or sideways from its fellow fingers, the energy represented by the estranged finger is powerful, but is not assimilated into the person's personality. For example, a Saturn finger held at an awkward angle indicates the person wants to accept some strict moral code but finds it does not fit smoothly into her life. An exception to this is if the Jupiter and Mercury fingers are held off to their respective sides. In such cases, the person is a free thinker who likes to speak and act her mind. If the separation is more pronounced on the nondominant hand, she dreams of distant seas while remaining forever in the bathtub. If the fingers are loosely spaced, things tend to run through the person's hand quickly, especially money. If the fingers are kept tight and close together, the person is overcautious and stingy with confidences and money.

The Long and the Short of It

The tension and posture of the fingers show the palmist how the person is using the energy available to her. With massage and changes in lifestyle, the tensions can be relaxed and postures changed. The length of the fingers cannot be changed, however, so the meaning of the finger length should be seen as one of the "givens" in a person's life which she should see as an asset since she is unable to change it. (Just remember, a long shapely finger is not always a sign of a kind personality.) Long fingers are well suited to detailed work and unless persuaded otherwise tend to be nitpickers. Short fingers deal more with the overall view. Executives and managers with short fingers and square palms are nearly guaranteed success, since they are practical and can see the whole picture. Their assistants should have long fingers so they can remember all the details with which their bosses can't be bothered.

This young woman has long, graceful fingers on a longish palm. Notice also that the top joints are longer than the middle ones, so she enjoys mental work.

Finger length is usually gauged in terms of the Saturn finger's length compared to the length of the palm. Saturn is usually 3/4 to 7/8 the length of the palm. That means if you divide the palm in half and divide one of the halves in half, the Saturn finger is as long as the distance to the bottom half, or a bit longer. Remember that a long hand can be composed of a long palm and short fingers, so don't confuse the two. If the Saturn is longer than 7/8 of the palm and the other fingers are proportional to it, then the fingers are considered long. If Saturn is shorter than 3/4, the fingers are short. As you read many hands you'll develop an eye for finger length and you won't have to figure it out every time, but in the beginning it's advisable to check every hand with this system.

Not Your Type?

Palmistry is separated into two areas—analysis of the hand itself, which is called *chirognomy*, and *chiromancy*. Chirognomy is the study of the form of hands and fingers. Chiromancy is the analysis of the lines, mounts and marks. You determine the shape of the hand by checking the shape of the palm. Sometimes it helps to connect the bottom of each finger with an imag-

THE SEVEN HAND TYPES OF d'ARPENTIGNY

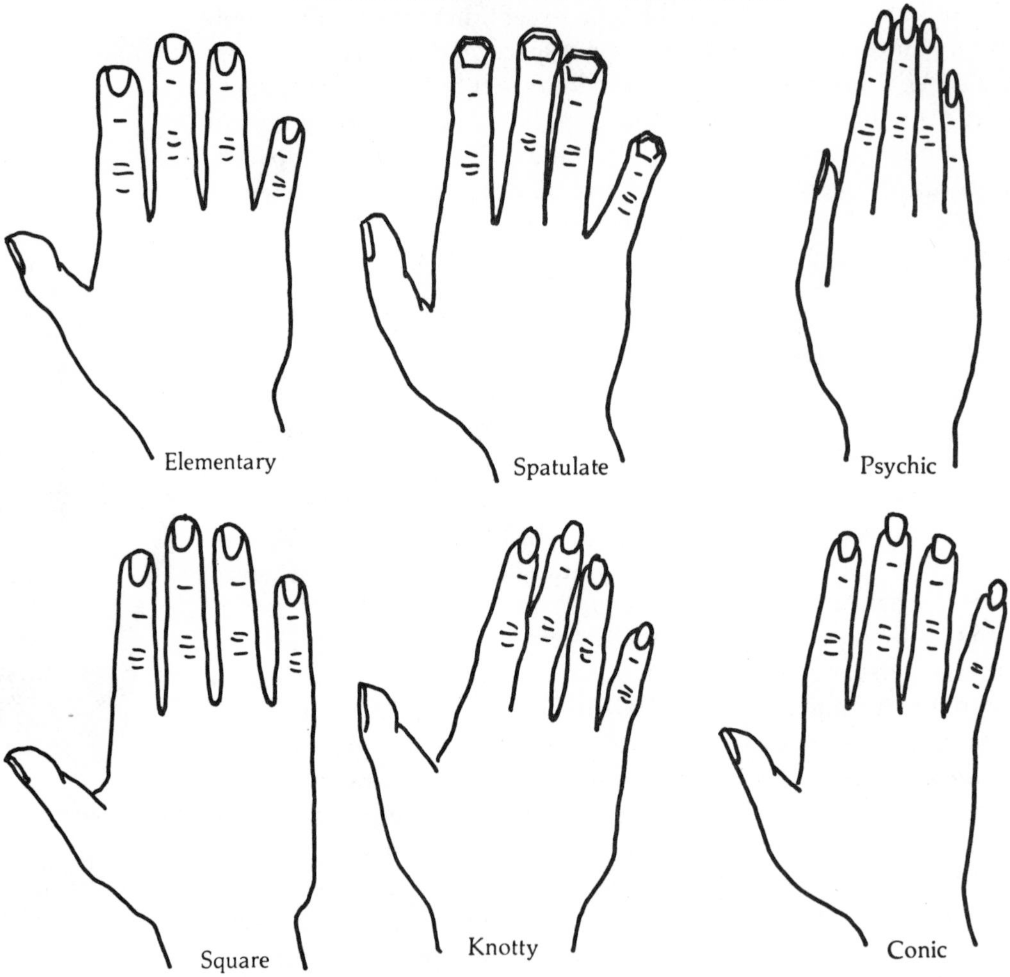

Elementary

Spatulate

Psychic

Square

Knotty

Conic

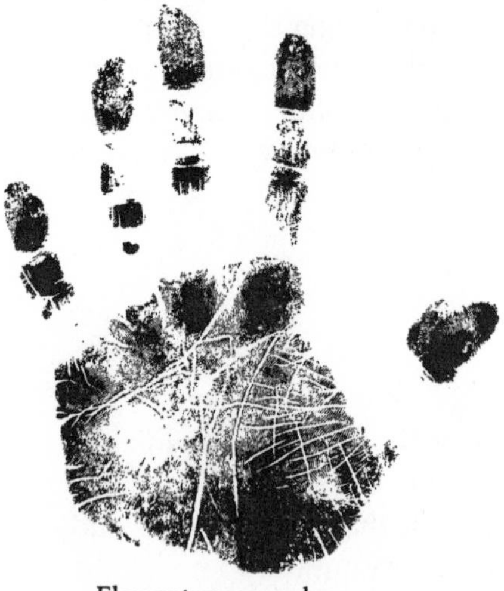

Elementary, my dear,
elementary!

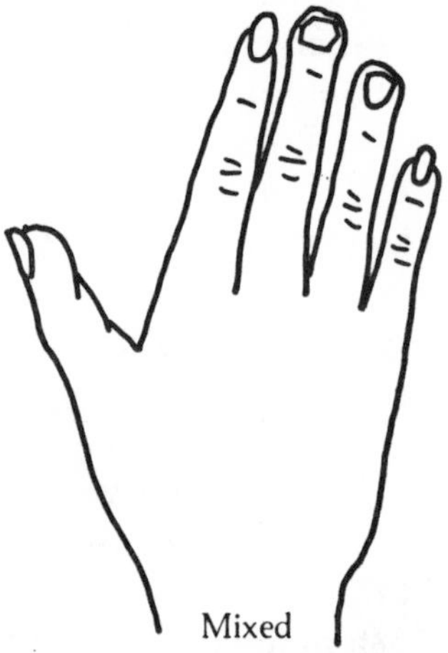

Mixed

inary line and see what shape pops out. As you read more hands and corroborate your readings with information from your subjects, it will become easier for you to spot types. Since pure examples of any type exist only in books like this, I shall present the most plausible among the classification systems and suggest that you study them carefully and then forget them entirely, so that you will be able to intuitively classify the general type of hand without agonizing over whether it's conical or spatulate. It is what it is, and although people whose hands are similar in shape often have similar temperaments, all classification systems are to be used only as general guidelines.

The first system to be widely accepted was that of d'Arpentigny. He saw six hand types: the elementary, spatulate, conic, square, knotty and psychic. He also allowed a mixed category for those which didn't fit into any of the pure types.

The *elementary* hand is squarish with short stubby fingers and few lines. He said it is unlikely you will find an elementary hand in a developed country, because such hands are found only among primitive people. This earned him big points in the Third World.

Spatulate or active hands are those which are narrower either at the base or near the fingers. They indicate the same thing as spatulate fingertips, namely that the person is impulsive, independent and creative. One fine point is that if the hand is broader at the base the person is more active, and will enjoy activities like trekking in the Himalayas or photographing the underbelly of a charging elephant. If the hand is more spatulate near the fingers, then the creativity is more mental, involving unusual concepts and ideas.

Conic or artistic hands are slightly tapered at the base of the palm and at the base of the fingers. People with conical hands are better followers than leaders, the Gertrude Steins of the world who support the efforts of others without creating much themselves. They are sensitive, helpful souls.

Square or useful hands are of equal width at the base and finger ends. They show a practical, rational nature. Square handed folks make good businessmen, and are competent and responsible. They can cope.

Knotty hands. Knotty hands? D'Arpentigny meant hands whose finger and knuckle joints are knotty, and claimed that they show a philosophical nature. He did not mention that hands of any shape can have knotty joints and not all arthritic people are philosophical.

Psychic or idealistic hands are long, thin and narrow, and are usually accompanied by pointed fingers. People with these hands are painfully idealistic; and energy flows through those pointed fingers so easily that they are too easily swayed or injured by influences from their environment.

Since it is frequently difficult to differentiate between a slightly conic hand and one that's a little spatulate, and since any shaped hand can be knotty, it's easy to see d'Arpentigny allowed a mixed category: Nearly everyone is in it.

The distinguished English palmist, Fred Gettings, prefers a fourfold division of hands which corresponds to the four elements—fire, air, water and earth—which are basic to astrology. The practical hand is ruled by earth; the intuitive hand is ruled by fire; the sensitive hand is ruled by water; and the intellectual hand is ruled by air. Each planet in the zodiac is ruled by one of these elements, but the element of the person's zodiac sign is not necessarily the same as the element of the hand. This is because the sign of the person's birth month is not the only determinant of her character. The position of the moon and other planets at the time of birth might combine to make her more fire-oriented even though she was born in an earth-ruled month. The zodiac signs and their elements are:

Earth	Taurus	Virgo	Capricorn
Fire	Aries	Leo	Sagittarius
Water	Pisces	Cancer	Scorpio
Air	Aquarius	Gemini	Libra

Gettings describes the *earth/practical* hand as having a square palm and, usually, short fingers. It is heavy, solid and has few lines. The person's character is like the character of earth—solid, supportive, practical, and productive. Despite an outward coolness and reliability, these people, like the earth, can have fiery subterranean impulses. Unless they are permitted to plod along as their inner natures dictate they are likely to erupt into fits of volcanic temper. Gettings mentions three factors which can lighten the heavy earth hand—skin texture, fingers and lines. If the skin is smooth, the fingers long or pointed, or the lines fine and numerous, then the stolid aspects of the earth character have mingled with more volatile and sensitive tendencies. This creates a complex type who has innate conflicts between various aspects of her personality. Gettings feels that earth types are best married to other earthlings as boring and dependable as themselves, or to a nice water type since, as every child knows, earth and water mix well.

The *intuitive* or *fire* hand has a long palm and short fingers. It is flexible and looks lively, with many fine lines covering the palmar surface. Like fire itself, fire types can have a warming, enlivening influence on their surroundings, be fast moving and changeable with the wind, and can sear and destroy when out of control. Many artists are fire types, as the abundance of energy and fine nervous lines on their hands provides them with a lot of self to express. Although fire types are frequently quite brilliant, they're not cool thinkers. Their intelligence is more often used to justify elaborate ideas to

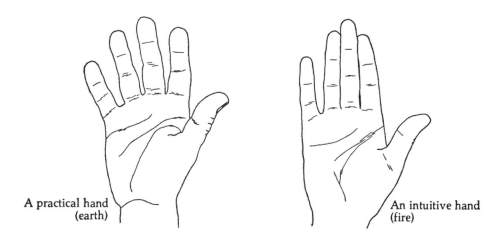

A practical hand
(earth)

An intuitive hand
(fire)

which they are emotionally attached. They're exciting to be around, although earth types are easily tired by the fire types' bursts of enthusiasm and sudden changes of interest. Fire types do not take well to authority. They generally feel suffocated by water types and bored by earth types. Air types are more to their liking, since the two of them can combine to roam the world as an ever-increasing fireball.

The *sensitive* or *water* hand has a long palm and long fingers. It is soft and flexible and seems quite refined. The skin texture is often so smooth that it looks like the surface of a pool. Both the hand shape and the interpretation are most similar to d'Arpentigny's conic hand. Water can be refreshing, reflective, restful. It has no form of its own, but takes its form from whatever is containing it. When whipped up by the wind or left unsupported by the earth, water can be an annihilator, but if left quietly on its own it will never move, either to destroy or to create. The most it can do is evaporate. Water people are a bit like this. They are more prone to receiving information, both from their companions and from their own unconscious minds, than they are to putting it out. Receptivity is a virtue as long as it's balanced by an occasional action. Unfortunately, action is a big problem for water types. They are always on the verge of doing something. They are emotional creatures, but they rarely act on their feelings; they'd rather wallow. A water type and a complex earth type can be happy together, as the imaginativeness of the water type livens up the earthling and the income of the earthling keeps the water type well contained. Water types turn to frightened steam and drift away when confronted by strong fire types.

The *intellectual* or *air* hand has a square palm and long fingers. The skin is very fine. The lines, although faint, seem less confused than those of a water or fire type. Air is the medium through which all communication passes, and most air types are involved with communications-related fields. Without air we would all die, yet it has no particular grounding point. Air is difficult to contain because it's everywhere. Do you know anyone who matches

31

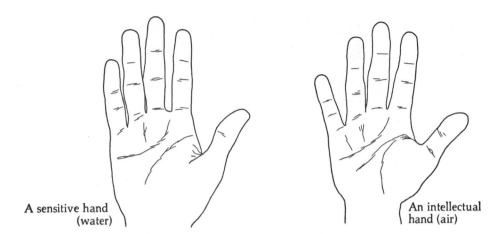

A sensitive hand
(water)

An intellectual
hand (air)

this description? Air types are conceptually oriented, curious about everything and eager to tell others about the things they've discovered. Their main weakness is in their limited emotionality and lack of grounding. Although their long fingers allow them to do highly detailed work, their ideas often bear no relation to the needs of the physical world. They're just interesting ideas. Air types love to put things in order, but their interest in pure order leads them to forget that other types take a heartfelt pleasure in a little disarray. They should be reminded to listen to their hearts and to relate their activities to the real world. They are gentle, interesting, and pleasant, and make good partners for fire types.

Dr. Charlotte Wolff combines the systems of Carl Gustav Carus, a German morphologist, and Kretschmer, a German psychiatrist, into an intriguing and useful system of hand classification. Carus devised his system in 1848. He postulated that there are four main body types, and that each type is associated with a specific type of personality and palm.

Kretschmer expanded this into a system of four constitutional types. Carus realized that the hand has two main functions, grasping and touching. He divided all hands into two groups, the *prehensile* or grasping group whose form is best suited for picking things up, and the *tactile* or touching group whose form is best suited for receiving sensations. He subdivided the prehensile group into *elementary* and *motoric* hands and the tactile group into the *sensitive* and the *psychic*. Kretschmer's system of body types included sketches of the nervous system, endocrine balance and temperament of each type. In some cases he's very accurate but his system is not useful for classifying everyone, since it places overdeveloped athletic people and deformed amorphous people into two of the four groups. That means 50 percent of humanity is either Arnold Schwarzenegger or Quasimodo. We'll retain the correlation between specific body types, hand types, and endocrine imbalances, because these have been verified by subsequent medical research.

Using Carus' distinction between the prehensile and the tactile types, Dr. Wolff noted three main groups of hands, *elementary*, *motoric*, and *sensitive*. Elementary and motoric are in the prehensile (grasping, acting) group, and the sensitives are alone in the tactile area. Naturally, every hand performs both functions; these groups show which function predominates. The Carus system is extremely useful in helping you judge the basic hand type and temperamental leanings of the person for whom you're reading. In places it matches Gettings' four elements system, and the two systems can easily be used in tandem. Wolff subdivided the prehensile group into two pairs: *elementary simple*, which roughly corresponds to Gettings' earth hand, and *elementary irregular*; and *motoric bony*, which might link up with the fire hand, and *motoric fleshy*. The sensitives she separated into *sensitive small* and *sensitive long*.

The *elementary simple* hand is large, muscular, and rather inflexible, with a few strong simple lines, a stout, powerful thumb, a strong mount of Venus, and shortish fingers. Those with these hands are good-natured, plodding, simple people who tolerate a lot of pressure before they blow up. Because of their slow natures, they are inclined to have problems with circulation in later life, and they tend to hypothyroidism. They work steadily and slowly, and are useful people to have around.

The *elementary irregular* hand has the same basic shape but carries unusual marks such as short, cruel-looking thumbs, overdeveloped mounts of Venus, and X's etched across the foreheads. Earlier writers refer to these marks as "atavistic," or "degenerate," but I try to see them as signs that this person was given distinct limitations at birth. Encourage her to do the best with what she has. The elementary irregular group contains two opposite sorts of people, according to Dr. Wolff. Those with tiny thumbs and monstrous mounts are likely to be "social misfits, habitual criminals, idiots, and madmen." They're also likely to be feebleminded. The others are likely to be hypersensitive, emotionally unbalanced, brilliant neurotics.

The *motoric bony* hand has a strong palm sprouting bony fingers. The Venus mount is well developed, indicating that action in the material world appeals to this person. The hand generally has many lines, showing that the person is a nervous, complex character. The thumb is long and graceful. This hand is usually found on tall, slender people who love to be in motion. Such people's interests are diverse, so diverse that they are often torn between their desire to be charging down Park Avenue at lunch hour and having themselves locked into meditation cells. They have an excellent sense of people's needs and thoughts, and are witty and articulate. They're prone to hyperthyroidism, which is why they often seem to be "up." Although their intellectual interests are wide, they prefer action to thought. Wolff describes them as "divided between the desire to escape and the desire to participate in human affairs."

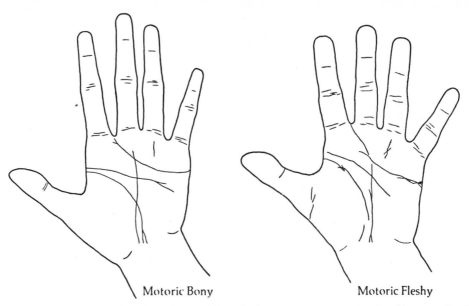

Motoric Bony   Motoric Fleshy

The *motoric fleshy* hand is broad and fleshy, as are the bodies to which these hands are attached. The thumb is large and forceful and the fingers are stout. These people may be slow, but everything they do is done right. Because of this natural slowness, they are prone to circulatory problems and have slight hypothyroid tendencies. Everyone should have at least one parent with motoric fleshy hands. They are patient, kindhearted, extroverted, wise, slow to anger, and they enjoy protecting the weak. Because of their natural stability and unwillingness to hurry, they make excellent corporate executives, statesmen and tribal patriarchs.

In the tactile group we find the *sensitive small* hand, which is characterized by a small, longish palm and short fingers. The muscles are weak and the mount of Luna is frequently elongated. All this shows that this hand is more open to receiving impressions than it is to acting on them. The characteristics of a sensitive small hand match those of a stereotypical weak woman, so the hand type is traditionally associated with women, even though many sensitive intellectual males also have sensitive small hands. This type has a delicate constitution and is hypersensitive to outside influences. The receptivity which is its virtue is also its weakness, because influences from the environment crowd in to form a sensory overload. These people are happiest in a calm, stable environment. They are prone to allergic illnesses and to chronic low energy levels. A small sensitive type and a motoric fleshy type would certainly make a good match.

The *sensitive long* hand has a long palm and graceful, tapering fingertips. This is the type of hand you've seen draped across the laps of many exquisite old paintings. The hand is weak, fragile and thin, and the palm is filled with fine webbed lines. It is so delicate that one hesitates to give it a firm handshake for fear it will crumble. This is d'Arpentigny's "psychic" hand, with a delicate nervous constitution and an excessive love of unearthly ideals. Since sitting demurely with aristocratic hands draped in the lap has gone out of

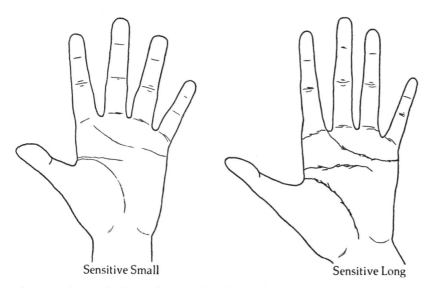

Sensitive Small   Sensitive Long

style, people with these lovely hands often suffer from their attempts to adapt to the real world. They are generally depressed and unable to snap out of it. Anything related to art or mysticism has their devoted attention, although their lack of grounding makes it difficult for them to succeed at being artists or mystics. Although many spiritual mediums have hands of this type, a sensitive long hand is no guarantee of psychic abilities. It is more likely a sign of painful idealism and dilettantism in religion and the arts.

Every hand is unique, so you will never see a perfect example of a type. Each of the three systems just presented (d'Arpentigny's five shapes; Gettings' four elements; and Carus' three groups with their subgroups) are useful in certain situations. Study this section and the accompanying illustrations carefully and then let your inner voice guide you in your readings. It's my experience that one hand will immediately strike me as "motoric bony" while another will say, "I'm conic." A system of classification is nothing but a mental grid laid onto the wonderful diversity of reality. All of these hand-type systems overlap, so breathe deeply, love the person you're reading for, and use what works best for you in each situation. Calling a hand "fire" or "sensitive small" is basically a prop to divert your intellectual mind while your intuition goes to work. Use whatever system works for you as you cultivate a feel for different hands.

By now you're pretty familiar with the hands you're reading. You've gotten a general feel for their tensions, their shapes, the shape of their fingertips, the character of the thumb, their color, temperature, flexibility, and their wetness or dryness. Without even looking at the lines or mounts, you know whether the person's artistic energy is being squashed by her moralism, whether she is decisive or willful, and whether she washed her hands before coming for the reading. With all that as a foundation, you are ready to look at the mounts and markings.

3

Mounts and Markings

Mighty Mounts, Vapid Valleys

A mount is an area of the palm itself which is usually bordered by lines or fingers. Mounts function as reservoirs of energy; when they stand out strikingly from the palm, they are called "high" or "strong" mounts and mean that the person has oodles of the energy represented by that part of the palm. For example, the mount of Venus represents physical energy, sensuality and sexuality. If the mount of Venus is plump and lush, watch for passion galore and love of all things touchable. If you see a round Venus mount on a timid type, don't believe the facade; whisk him off to a disco and you'll see his wanton side.

A mount is not always a mound. If the palm is flat, or even hollowed out, then the energy represented by that part of the hand is dried up or repressed. It can, however, be built up by consciously redirecting energy into whatever areas lack vitality, and through activities which will rebuild that energy. Back to the mount of Venus example—(Venus examples are always popular)—if you find that your Venus has gone flat, have sex more often. If that is unfeasible, take up other activities which will bring together your physical vitality and your enjoyment of the delicious assortment of sensual experiences constantly available to you. All experiences that don't go on inside your head are sensual experiences—pick out the ones you like and keep them up!

Occasionally you will see lines on your hands change after you've made some change in your lifestyle or in your attitudes about yourself. These changes appear gradually. However, the level of the mounts changes more quickly than the form of the lines. If you don't believe this (and I wouldn't blame you if you didn't), check it out for yourself. Look at your hands now. Note the height and firmness of the various sections of your hands. Are you rested? Tired? Feeling tuned in to your body? Try to remember the way your hands look now. Look at them again later this evening or in a few days, particularly at times when you feel extremely good or exceptionally tired. Now do you believe me? While you're looking, you might also see the color of the skin on your palm and even the marks on the lines changing from red to black to dark, depending on your mood. Don't worry about marks too much at this point; we'll get to those later in this chapter.

The Eight Major Mounts and What They Do

There are eight major mounts on each hand. All of them are named after Greek or Roman gods or goddesses, just like the fingers. In fact, four of the mounts have the same patron gods and goddesses as the fingers that lie above them; They are Jupiter, Saturn, Apollo and Mercury. If you recall your Greek mythology you'll know that Jupiter's the jovial fellow hurling thunder bolts from Olympus; Saturn is the pensive one holding the sickle; Apollo's playing his tune on the lyre and Mercury is dashing off on his winged sandals to deliver a telegram from the gods to the mortals. As with the fingers, the significance of the fingers and mounts named after the gods is correlated with the attributes of the gods themselves.

You will probably remember that Jupiter, also known as Zeus, was the king of the gods. He dispensed justice and lightning storms, so his finger represents ambition and the desire to be charismatic. The power can be religious or secular, depending on the rest of the hand. Saturn never quite recovered from the loss of the universe, so he became philosophical and slightly morbid. In Roman myth, Saturn's daughter is Veritas, or truth. This is one of Saturn's good points—he also represents scientific investigation and the desire to know and do what is right. Apollo, god of the sun, was the patron of medicine and the arts; his refined aesthetic style was the vogue of the Classical world, and his finger is still associated with the love of beauty. Finally, little Mercury, the Greek Hermes, was the messenger of the gods and intermediary between heaven and earth. He was the patron of thieves and merchants. Now he represents skill at speech, commerce and diplomacy, or the desire to communicate one's inner goals through verbal expression.

The mounts under the fingers—Jupiter, Saturn, Apollo and Mercury—are storehouses of the energy that each finger represents. Imagine the energy flowing from the mounts of Venus and Luna and being filtered through them until it flows out into the world through the fingertips. If you look at your hand (or someone else's) and see that one of these mounts seems particularly thick, you can conclude that you have a strong capacity or desire to express yourself in the activities governed by that particular finger or mount. For instance, if your mount of Apollo is noticeably higher than the others, then you have creative urges which you would like to express. If the fullness continues the length of the finger so that the finger *and* the mount are full, then you're actually moving that energy out. Otherwise it's a storehouse that has yet to be tapped. This is like having a brand new sports car and being afraid to drive it.

It is energy that makes the mounts swell up. In addition to examining the height of the mounts, note their firmness. High, firm mounts are ideal, as they indicate the person is using the abundant energy at his disposal. High (that is, thick) flabby mounts indicate too much love of comfort, a sort of all-inclusive gluttony. If a person's flabby hand shows you that life is not performing up to his standards, you can bet his lack of success stems not from lack of ability, but from lack of direction, from self-pity, or from laziness. Don't be too sympathetic. Flat, firm mounts always indicate a cool disposition. In addition to the mounts under the fingers, the other major mounts are Venus, Luna, Upper Mars, and Lower Mars.

Venus

Venus was the desired and desiring goddess of love who was born from ocean foam during a Greek myth. She was known as the goddess of beauty, the mother of love, queen of laughter and was the patroness of courtesans. The mount of Venus is an enormous reservoir of physical vitality, particularly of vitality for sexual and sensual pleasures. Someone with a well-

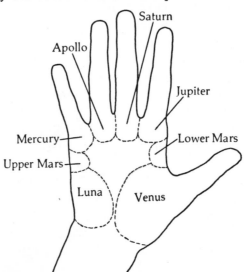

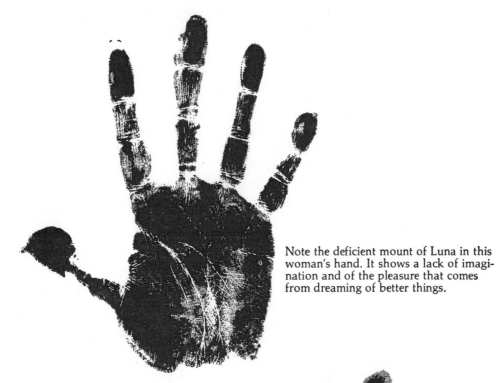

Note the deficient mount of Luna in this woman's hand. It shows a lack of imagination and of the pleasure that comes from dreaming of better things.

In the compact hand of Dr. Zev Wanderer, noted psychologist and author of *Letting Go*, we see a powerful mount of Venus bounded by an adventurous and deep life line. Also note that the thumbtip is well-formed, which shows his ability to follow through on the tasks he sets for himself.

rounded mount of Venus is likely to have a frank, forceful appreciation of all sensory delights, and the stamina necessary to indulge in them.

Luna

Luna is the goddess of the moon. The moon is associated with the tides, so it is linked with long voyages. Luna is also known as the patroness of the occult and spiritual arts and is associated with all parts of the mind that stay hidden during the day, that is, with the unconscious and the world of dreams. When Luna gets out of control, she is linked with lunacy or the incapacity to control the imagination or to differentiate between fantasy and reality.

The exact significance of lines appearing on Luna differs according to the origin of the lines. Fate lines or life lines which end or send branches to Luna are less likely to imply craziness than are head lines which descend to her. A life line ending on Luna implies travel or great restlessness, and a fate line there implies a career in which intuition is used regularly. This includes those which are directly related to mystical or poetic pursuits.. Head lines that sink deep into the moon imply that the imagination is likely to run amok. I once read the palms of a group of patients in a psychiatric ward, and found the majority of them had steeply sloping head lines. For more on medical correlations between insanity and signs on the palm, see Chapter 5. The deeper into Luna any line descends, the more of the moon's uncanny energy the person feels.

Mars Mounts

There are two mounts of Mars. Both represent courage and the aggressive spirit associated with Mars, the Roman god of war. Upper Mars, which is found just under the mount of Mercury, is like an underground reservoir of stubborn perseverance. When someone with a strong mount of Upper Mars digs in his heels and refuses to surrender, his opponents had better prepare for a long siege. People with strong mounts of Upper Mars often appear to be adaptable and easygoing, but just oppose them in something they really want to do and you'll see them clinging to their goals like lichen clings to a rock.

People with strong mounts of Lower Mars are less discreet about their stubbornness. Lower Mars is found between the head line and the thumb, tucked into the mount of Venus. In Roman mythology, Venus and Mars were enraptured lovers, and they are still side by side here on the hand. A strong mount of Lower Mars means that this person will *actively* resist those who obstruct his will or those with whom he disagrees.

The Quadrangle, the Mystic Triangle, and the Ring of Solomon

If you take away all the mounts on the hand, the leftover area will be the quadrangle or the plain of Mars. This is colloquially known as the "hollow of the palm." A deeply hollowed quad generally signifies an extremely sensitive and high-strung nature.

The quadrangle is also the site of the acclaimed Mystic Triangle. This triangle, which is found between the head and heart lines in the center of the palm, implies skill in the occult or psychic arts. If one side of the triangle is formed by the fate line, then the person's entire life will be influenced by his aptitude for psychic skills. A lot of people want to think that they have Mystic Triangles, but we accept only the true product; there must be a complete three-sided triangle here or all you have is a few lines of influence meandering across the quadrangle. True Mystic Triangles are relatively rare.

The mount of Luna and the Mystic Triangle are both related to the use of intuition; the difference is that although someone with a strong mount of Luna has clear access to his intuition, that intuition may pop up randomly, outside of his conscious control, or it may be used in diverse activities such as business, healing or creative arts. In someone with a true Mystic Triangle, the intuitive powers are likely to be refined into sensible activities like telepathy or astral travel. I once met a conservative English stockbroker who had a perfect Mystic Triangle. He pooh-poohed everything I asked him about psychic experiences, until, long after the roast beef, Yorkshire pudding and wine had been drowned in after-dinner brandy, he confessed, at his wife's urging, that he often astral traveled during his sleep.

Sometimes the space which would be taken up by the Mystic Triangle is filled by a distinct cross, which is called, not surprisingly, the Mystic Cross. This cross has roughly the same significance as the Mystic Triangle, but since the cross is generally a less auspicious sign than the triangle, a person with a Mystic Cross will have to work harder to make his powers useful. Still, he'll have an easier time than someone who has neither of these marks.

The other marks that appear on the mounts are the *Girdle of Venus* and the *Ring of Solomon*. The Girdle of Venus is an arch extending from the space between Saturn and Jupiter to the space between Apollo and Mercury. It represents tremendous sensitivity. This heightened awareness usually leads to greater concern and compassion in all the person's activities. However, on a hand with very weak or chained heart and head lines or a weak thumb, the potential for sensitivity can deteriorate into extreme touchiness. Often you will see a Girdle of Venus that is still half-formed or is composed of a series of little lines in the approximate shape of the Girdle. People with "Girdlettes" are working on themselves, trying to become more aware of the effects of their actions on their brethren; at least they're not as touchy as some with fully formed Girdles.

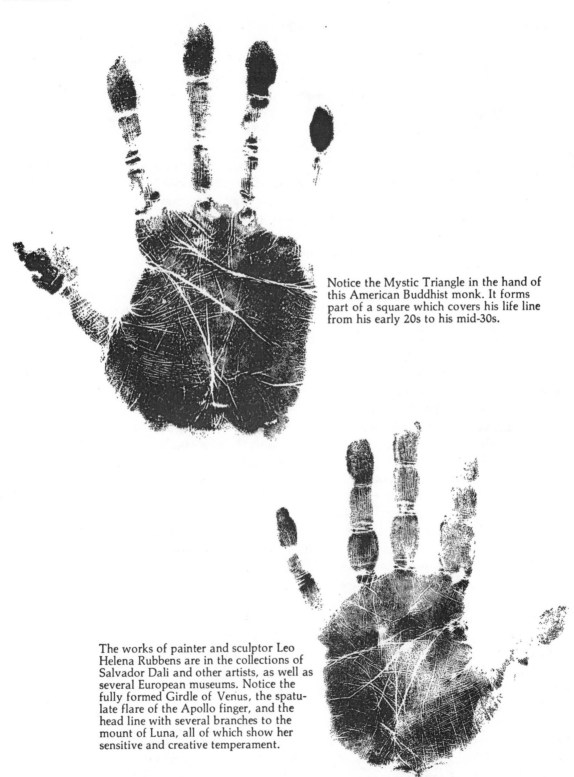

Notice the Mystic Triangle in the hand of this American Buddhist monk. It forms part of a square which covers his life line from his early 20s to his mid-30s.

The works of painter and sculptor Leo Helena Rubbens are in the collections of Salvador Dali and other artists, as well as several European museums. Notice the fully formed Girdle of Venus, the spatulate flare of the Apollo finger, and the head line with several branches to the mount of Luna, all of which show her sensitive and creative temperament.

Another rare and intriguing mark on the palm is the Ring of Solomon, which is a semicircle found just under the Jupiter finger. In the Bible, Solomon was supposed to be the wisest king, so his Ring gives the bearer a charismatic presence that is associated with spiritual leadership.

Marks and The Rivers

Imagine you have been commissioned to make a navigational map of a river. You are in an airplane scudding low over the surface. You look ahead, and see that for a few miles the surface is smooth. Several minutes later, you hit the rapids. Foaming water hurls up branches and debris as the water spins in vicious whirlpools. A little further down, the rapids end abruptly and you come to a small island in the middle of the stream. This island divides the river into two separate, smaller rivers, each having half the energy of the full flow. You chart the other parts of the river by examining the surface of the water, checking the state of the riverbanks, looking for more islands, logjams, and by noting the many other differences in the color and condition of the water that tell an experienced navigator what to expect.

Every line on the hand is a river, and you are the pilot, charting and interpreting the subtle signals the river gives you. Any part of the hand can be touched by one or more of the marks you're about to learn, and you will be able to interpret those marks by noting where they appear on the hand and by listening to your intuition. *Marks represent obstructions or qualifications of the type of energy manifested on the line or mount on which they appear.* As you learn the marks, the process of interpreting them will become second nature.

Another thing that should become second nature to you is keeping your mouth shut until you've looked closely at the whole hand. Before making a final judgment on the meaning of a particular mark, be sure to see it in the context of the entire hand, noting whether the protective or negative influences implied by a particular mark are supported or limited by the force of other lines and marks on the hand. For example, a star is usually a very auspicious sign, but if it appears on a hand which is otherwise weak or full of chained lines, it would have to be a supernova to overcome the draining influences of the other parts of the hand.

Another thing about marks is that you don't *have* to have them. In fact, no one has all of them, and a lot of very happy people are padding about the earth without any special marks on their hands at all. Those who do have marks are likely to have some combination of these:

Dots   These are temporary blockages of energy. They may signify a depression if found on the head line or heart line, or indicate minor illnesses if found on the life line, or temporary career setbacks if found on the fate line. Ask your intuition about the exact reason for these minor hindrances.

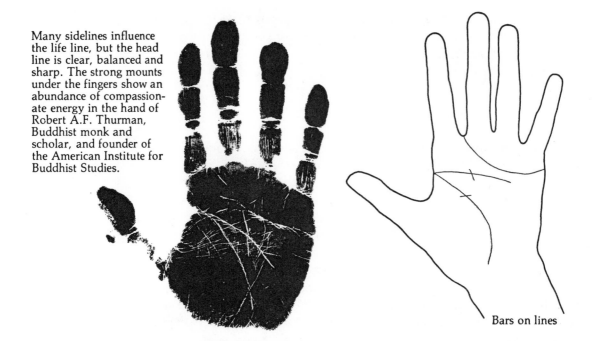

Many sidelines influence the life line, but the head line is clear, balanced and sharp. The strong mounts under the fingers show an abundance of compassionate energy in the hand of Robert A.F. Thurman, Buddhist monk and scholar, and founder of the American Institute for Buddhist Studies.

Bars on lines

Bars These are like serious logjams on the rivers of the lines. They indicate a more significant obstacle to the clear flow of energy through the line than do dots, and thus can signify more major illnesses or depressions or outside influences which temporarily obstruct the flow of energy in the area of the palm on which the bar is found.

Your intuition will help you interpret these marks. Sometimes a bar early in the life indicates a tragedy in the family. Bars in the fate line might indicate betrayal from a business colleague. Take a deep breath, put your attention in the center of your abdomen and ask for more details. If nothing comes to you immediately, don't worry about it. Continue with the reading.

Sidelines of Influence Occasionally a line will approach one of the major lines from the side and touch that line. There's nothing wrong with being oblique. If a line approaches from beside or slightly below a major line and does not cut directly through it, you have before you a *line of influence*, not a bar. These lines mean only that a major influence has entered the life. You can tell the type of influence by looking at the origin of the line of influence. See a line springing from the mount of Apollo and touching the heart line? Then you know that this person's heart has been touched by a love of art, or that he sometimes embroils himself in sticky emotional situations because he loves drama.

Islands Like islands in a river, islands in a line divide the flow of energy in two and thus weaken the line. Islands in the life line indicate a period of divi-

The island in the head line is accompanied by the island in the life line, signifying a period of division and ambivalence which affects the mental and daily life of this man. Fortunately, he has an inner life line which shields him from the worst effects of the islands.

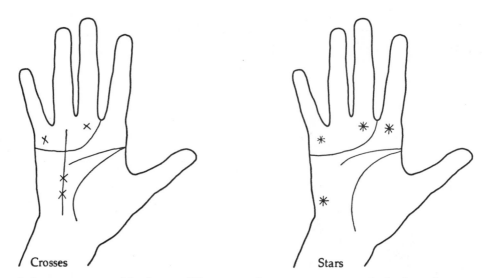

Crosses   Stars

ded energy or ambivalence. They can also represent a period when the person wanted to do one thing but was forced by circumstance to do another.

For instance, I once read the hands of the widow of a well-known millionaire. Her life line divided into an island somewhere in her early twenties and continued in two parts for a little more than an inch, or in human time until she was in her late thirties. In this case, it seemed that she had taken part of her natural vivacity and "gone underground," showing one part of herself to the world but keeping most of her true interests hidden. She agreed with my interpretation, and said that being the wife of a prominent business figure had indeed forced her to hide some of the more exuberant and creative aspects of her character. She loved her husband, but she felt that in many ways she had become *herself* again after his death. This is one example of how the precise explanation of a particular mark depends on the intuitive feeling the mark gives you.

Crosses   Crosses on the lines generally mean the same thing as crosses across an answer on a test. Wrong. They are signs that the person's desires are being opposed, which is even worse than the obstruction implied by bars. The type of opposition depends on the place on the hand where the cross is found. For instance, if it is on the head line, the person runs into some health problem or problem of circumstance which inhibits him from thinking clearly. Once again, a lone cross does not an awful life make, but it is a sign of difficulty at whatever point the cross appears.

Stars   Stars are as good as crosses are bad. Except when they appear under the mount of Saturn, they indicate good fortune and success in whatever area of life is signified by the part of the hand on which they appear. The best place to find a star, other than in the sky, is on the mount of Jupiter. Here they foretell a life of fame and fortune beyond most people's dreams.

Squares   Squares do not always fall within a line; they are more likely to be spread over a particular line or area of the hand. They are marks of protection and preservation from harm. If there is a break in any of the lines, and the break is covered by a square, then the person will be protected from feeling the full negative effects of whatever mischance, whether it be illness, accident or freak-out, that the break represents. Some people say that squares are signs of preservation by some spiritual force; others say it springs from the person's own inner resources. Your interpretation should depend on the message you receive from the individual hand.

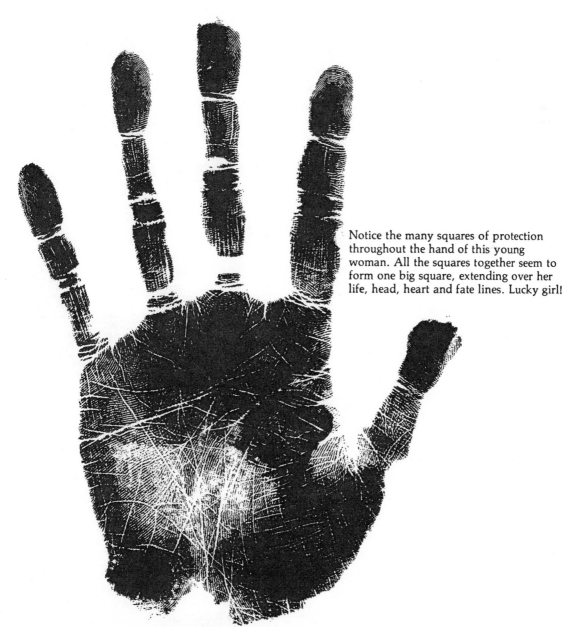

Notice the many squares of protection throughout the hand of this young woman. All the squares together seem to form one big square, extending over her life, head, heart and fate lines. Lucky girl!

There is one startling thing about hands on which squares appear: The squares last only as long as they are needed. I have seen many hands, including my own, on which one of the lines had a break in it or became extremely weak and in which a square extended throughout the period where the main line was weak, broken or tasseled. At the point in the line (and therefore in the life) when the pain that caused the break was healed, the square just melted away. A protective square is like a fairy godmother who stands by until Cinderella marries the prince and then vanishes in a wisp of smoke.

Triangles   It is much more rare to find a triangle over a line than to find a square. In general, triangles have a calming or rationalizing influence on the energy of the mount on which they are found. For example, on the mount of Venus, triangles imply restraint of passion. On Jupiter, this calmness allows the person to have more powerful influence on those around him. (Often, people have more faith in an unruffled personality.) The triangle on the mount of Saturn is especially auspicious, signifying exceptional skill in mystical or occult pursuits.

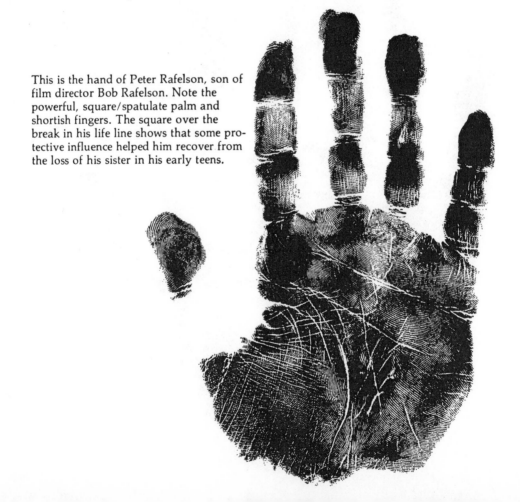

This is the hand of Peter Rafelson, son of film director Bob Rafelson. Note the powerful, square/spatulate palm and shortish fingers. The square over the break in his life line shows that some protective influence helped him recover from the loss of his sister in his early teens.

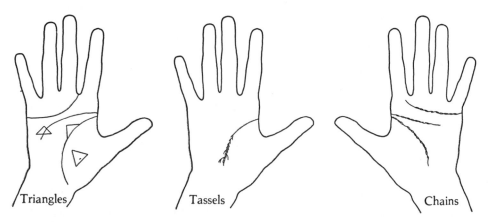

Triangles | Tassels | Chains

Grids Grids mark an amplification of the skills or tendencies associated with the mounts on which they are found. Those of you with grids should beware of having too much of a good thing, because the energies of the mount are excited to the point where they may be hard to control. Also, the energy is not channeled as it is on lines, so it tends to stay in the gridded section of the palm and make trouble. That means, for example, that if you have grids on your mount of Venus, your passion for the voluptuous is hard to control. Grids on the mount of Venus also warn of a possible physical weakness: Watch out for those contagious "bugs" that we all know and hate. When found on the mount of Apollo, grids mean an excessive exuberance for things artsy which could lead to dilettantism at the expense of true artistic production.

Chained or tasseled lines Remember when you were making your map of the river? If you come to a part of the river where waves slice against the rocks and jetties cut into the river, you know that the water is in an uproar. Similarly, if the lines are chained or broken up, the energy cannot flow freely and the power of the line is diminished. If the life line is chained, the person is likely to be nervous and full of disharmony. If you see a chained life line on a hand where other lines are in good shape, then this person's clear head and healthy heart are keeping his nerves under control; however, it's probably an uphill battle. If the heart line is chained, the person is insecure and easily hurt in love. If the head line is chained, it is hard for the person to remain focused on any subject; he is forever wandering into depressing or confused trains of thought.

Tasseled lines indicate a gradual weakening of the powers associated with the line. This is most often found in the life line, where a tasseling at the end indicates that the person's vitality wanes gradually as he approaches old age. This is no surprise; it's a rare person who has the good luck to run straight into death after a long and healthy life.

Wavy lines mean that the person is incapable of taking a direct route to anywhere.

Using the analogy of the river and line, you can interpret most of the changes or weaknesses you will find in lines on the palm. Your intuition will guide you where your intellect fails as long as you remember to put your attention in your center and listen carefully to what the palm and your center are asking you to say. If you've already made up your mind what you think or what impression you want to make on the person whose hands you are reading, you'll never get anywhere but deeper into embarrassment.

Color

Interpreting the color of the hands is a significant part of your hand reading. Hand hue can range from bluish pale to bright red. Significance of the color of the hands should be judged in the context of the natural color of the whole body. Black people can have healthy pink lines and white people can have black spots or dark lines.

A gray, pale line or hand indicates that the person is morose and disinterested in life. No matter how vigorous he could be, he just doesn't want to get enthusiastic. Encourage him to eat less sugar and get more exercise; it might help. If the lines are actually dark grey or black, this person is nursing anger and disappointment. Resentment would seep out if you squeezed this line. Darkness on lines is like sewage in pipes: It's only bad if it doesn't get removed. People with dark lines need an emotional Roto-Rooter, that is, they should be encouraged to get whatever is making them so angry out of their system. Suggest that they scream or shout, or go tell their mother they're not going to be an accountant anymore. Whatever it takes to get rid of the sludge, this person ought to do, since his clogged emotional pipes are not hurting anyone but himself.

Red lines always indicate an active and energetic nature, but depending on the context of the hand and on your intuitive response to the color, the redness can mean productive vigor or unproductive upsets. I'd rather have a red line than a black one, because at least it means that the life energies are in motion. Since red lines can mean anything from anger to zeal, you'll have to listen carefully to the breath in your center. Tune in there for more detail.

You might see your heart line turn red after a fight or even a rousing discussion with a loved one. You might see your fate line glow red after you've done something strongly associated with your career. Nevertheless, there are times when a red line definitely indicates passionate anger. Only the palm knows for sure, and it is conveying everything you need to know to your intuitive center. All you have to do is ask.

Another color variation is white puffy areas on or around certain parts of the line. Although they could appear anywhere, they are most likely to appear near the end of the heart line or on the marriage lines. These white puffs signify uncried tears or unfaced sadness. The only thing to make them go away is to cry those tears and get them out of your system. These areas are similar to dark lines in that they signify a block of emotional pain. The difference is that people with dark lines have hardened into their pain and decided their problems are insoluble or that the fault for their troubles rests with the world, whereas people with puffy areas around their heart lines still feel hurt and afraid that their grief will overwhelm them if they give it a chance to come out. Not true. Their grief will overwhelm them if they never really experience it, and it will probably make them sick in the process. I see dark, hard lines as being like hard, dry earth which would require a two-ton rototiller before it could be planted; white puffy areas are like plowed fields ready for planting and sprouting.

If you see a puffy area near a branch of the heart line heading up between Jupiter and Saturn, or if there is no line there at the moment but that space is taken up by a raised puffy white area, the person would like to be closer to people and has the capacity to move into closer intimate relations. Even though he is hopeful about future loves, a previous disappointment is holding him back. If the rest of the hand is fairly clear, this person will probably work out his fears by himself. When you see a puffy area, be as compassionate as possible in advising the person about how to deal with it. Obviously, if it were easy for him to express his emotions, he would have expressed them already.

Often, the phrase "uncried tears" will be enough to dampen this person's eyes, so unless you're willing to listen to the whole story and stay there until the catharsis is over, don't press him too much. Look at the entire hand and think carefully. Listen to your intuition. What would be best for this individual case? If the person has a strong mount of Mercury, indicating verbal ability, he might find release through writing a journal. Someone with a stronger Apollo might want to paint or strum his blues away. Someone with a well-developed mount of Luna can find comfort in religion or in his own intuition's advice, if you remind him to listen. Or, if you find someone who thinks all the above is a waste of time, point out the impracticality of keeping pain bottled up and the possibility of letting it out a little at a time without feeling silly. Some people confuse acting like a human being with acting like an idiot. Your sensible client might release his pain by going for long walks or jogging.

Now you know a little more about the gods of the mountains, and you can read the signs that the energy makes as it runs through the lines and bulges up under the mounts. As you chart the rivers and plains of the hands, you'll know how to read the assorted signs and you'll be able to predict when the rivers will get choppy. With a little background on the characteristics of the Greek gods who gave their names to the parts of the hands, you are in an even better position to synthesize the meaning of the various sections of the hands with the meaning of the markings unique to each hand. But you still ought to know the names of the river lines.

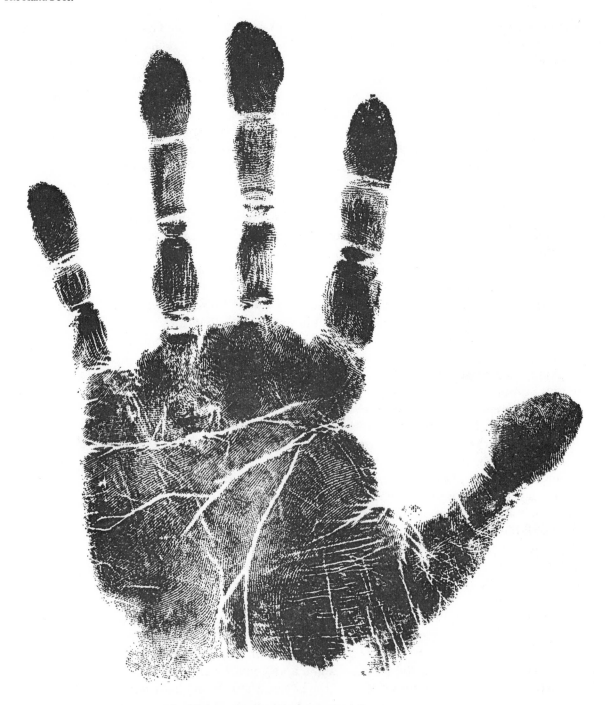

The life line is powerful and clear on the hand of singer and entertainer Paul McCarthy. Note the branch of the head line which pulls him into analytical thought whenever his imagination gets too restless.

4

What's My Line?

I don't know exactly how your childhood illnesses and adolescent heart-breaks came to be recorded on your hand, but I do know they're there. I (and many other palmists in the last few thousand years) have noticed that there are correlations between lines on the hand and the past, present, and probably the future of the person whose arm is connected to the hand.

Lines on the palm are rivers of energy
which can change as you change your life.

One more thing before proceeding: Please weigh *all* the signs in the hand before making any grand pronouncements. Negative factors in one part of the hand are often compensated by positive factors in another. Also, remind those trembling hands that lines and mounts occasionally change, and the only way to change your lines is from the inside out; that means changing your lifestyle or attitudes. My widowed mother's life line was fairly short until her late forties and then extended a full inch down her hand after she fell in love again and decided life was worth living after all. The same thing could happen to you.

Now let's suppose your friend's hand is nestled comfortably in yours and you are amazing her with your palm reading. You've taken a few deep breaths and have remembered the intuitive energy which is now coursing through your veins. You've looked at the shape of the hands and classified

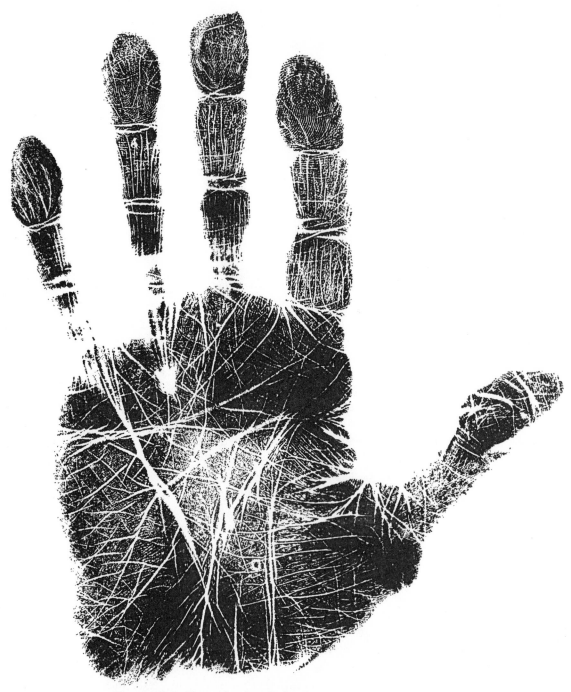

This 80-year-old man has hands electrically charged with lines of influence. Remember that this shows a sensitive and high-strung disposition, or you could spend all day trying to read each line!

54

them. You know the meanings of all the fingers and mounts. You know which of the fingers are tensed with blocked energy and which are relaxed. Your intuition and your intellect have been giving you tidbits of information. Now you are ready to examine the main lines.

Main Lines

There are three primary lines and a fourth one which is almost primary. The big three are the life line, the heart line and the head line. The almost-primary line is the fate line which appears in most, but not all, hands. I have never seen a hand or a print of a hand with no life line. Occasionally the head line and the heart line merge into one line which cuts the hand in half; that's the simian line, and is not science fiction.

The Life Line

The life line is the central line of the hand. On it are recorded all the major events of the life. It shows the level of physical vitality, the attitude toward travel and adventure, and gives a very rough idea of the probable length of the life. Length of life depends primarily on will to live and luck. The former is recorded on the line; the latter, who knows? Regardless of its length, a good strong life line can outweigh all kinds of unsavory marks elsewhere on the hand.

When trying to place events on the line in chronological order, consider the thumb end of the line as "birth." Figure the point at the bottom of the hand before the line begins to curve around the wrist as about 65 years old. A bit of nimble mental arithmetic will tell you that halfway down the life line is the point at which the person is 30-35 years old. Your intuition will give you more specific details if you're listening.

Let me reiterate that the end of the life line does not necessarily mean the end of life. I feel that palmists should *never* predict the age at which a person will die. The palmist might be wrong, and yet predictions of death plant insidious seeds of fear and self-fulfilling prophecy, even in people who "don't believe a word of it." When people ask you when they are going to die, simply assure them *that* they are going to die, but tell them the exact date is not for us mortals to know in advance.

At any rate, what's the use of thinking about death? Live life. Here are the main variations which you are likely to encounter on the life lines:

> *long, deep, and clear* indicates excellent vitality, minimal heartache, and an ability to be grounded in the physical world and cope with everyday life.

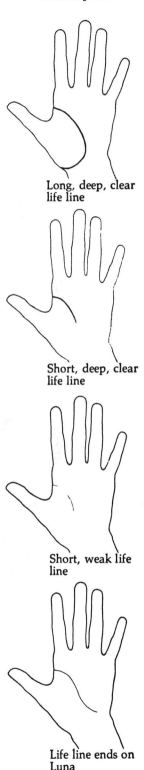

Long, deep, clear life line

Short, deep, clear life line

Short, weak life line

Life line ends on Luna

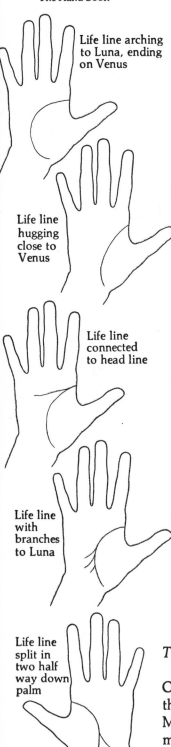

Life line arching to Luna, ending on Venus

Life line hugging close to Venus

Life line connected to head line

Life line with branches to Luna

Life line split in two half way down palm

short, deep, and clear indicates a very intense person; if combined with a sharply curving head line, this person is probably both intense and reckless.

short and weak means perpetually blase, and this person lacks involvement in the world outside herself.

ending on the mount of Luna shows a restless spirit, and this person will long for travel throughout her life. She may well settle or die in a country across the sea from where she was born.

arching wide across the hand toward Luna and ending close to the mount of Venus shows one who travels widely, but always returns home.

hugging very close to the thumb means she is timid, slightly conservative, and fond of domestic life.

connected to the head line means a person who is very close to family during youth. If the two lines run together for more than a third of the head line, it takes her until at least her mid-20's to become independent from her family. One effect of this long period of dependence is that she is cautious and reserved in making decisions and commitments throughout her life. Sometimes the two lines separate gradually, implying that she had to break away from her past in several short steps rather than one great leap.

branches from the life line in the direction of Luna mark individual voyages, and are quite simple to read; a long branch is a long journey; a short branch is a short journey.

splits in two about halfway down the palm signifies an exceptionally restless disposition; the person loves to roam. She may have the choice of moving overseas in middle age. If the line is in two parts of equal depth when you read it, she is still undecided about whether to go. Whichever branch of the line is strongest at the time the decision has to be made is probably the direction that she will take, that is, if the line closer to the thumb is stronger she'll stay, and if the Luna branch is stronger she'll go.

The Inner Life Line

Occasionally you see a line running parallel to the life line, toward the thumb side of the hand. This is known as the inner life line, or the line of Mars. It is always a sign of added strength and vitality. Sometimes it simply means physical vitality, and sometimes implies spiritual support or a companion who provides love and assistance. Consult your intuition about the precise meaning of this line.

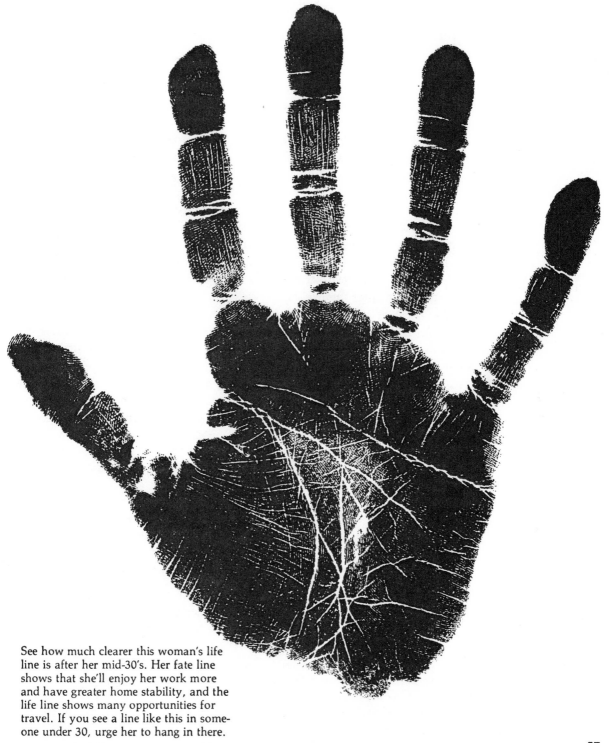

See how much clearer this woman's life line is after her mid-30's. Her fate line shows that she'll enjoy her work more and have greater home stability, and the life line shows many opportunities for travel. If you see a line like this in someone under 30, urge her to hang in there.

Regardless of whether this line represents a person, a creed, or simple brute strength, the line of Mars is a favorable sign. Particularly if the life line is weak or broken, the line of Mars can be a lifesaver, as the extra energy it provides can make the difference between life and death for a person whose vitality is weak or drained by illness.

The Heart Line

Since most people are fascinated by questions of emotions and love, pay special attention to this line. The heart line signifies attitudes toward love and intimacy. Marks on the heart line have the same significance as they do elsewhere on the palm. They represent different changes or obstructions, in this case, in the emotional life of the person. The overall form of the line tells you how the person handles herself in emotional affairs and tells you her basic attitudes toward emotional relationships. This line does not relate to marriage per se; rather it reflects the person's own feelings about involvement, which naturally affect her marriages, but such liaisons should be read on the marriage lines themselves.

Under the Mercury finger, the heart line represents the person's early emotional life. If it is chained, she felt insecure and unloved as a child and if it is strong, she felt bathed in love. Since nearly everyone's heart line begins under Mercury, its placement there does not tell us as much as the quality does. If the line does not extend all the way to the Mercury side of the palm, the person is not too deeply attached to anyone. At the other end of the line, the variations become more diverse. Note the length, direction and general condition of the line. The heart line can:

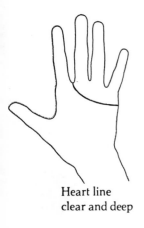

Heart line
clear and deep

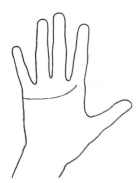

Heart line ends
deep in Jupiter

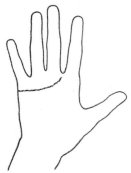

Weak, chained
heart line

run deep into Saturn, signifying idealism in emotional relationships. This person is looking for perfect people. Good luck.

terminate deep in Jupiter, indicating the person is passionate but somewhat self-centered in love. A person with a line like this can be devoutly loyal and possessive, but her primary interest is in what is good for herself.

end between Jupiter and Saturn, meaning the person has a realistic and mature attitude about emotional affairs. She knows how much she can reasonably expect from her love life, and is thus unlikely to be disappointed.

sometimes traverse the entire palm, implying a willingness to be involved with humanity in general, that is, to be nice to everyone and have many acquaintances. The main result of this is that the person is hesitant to commit herself to anyone in particular.

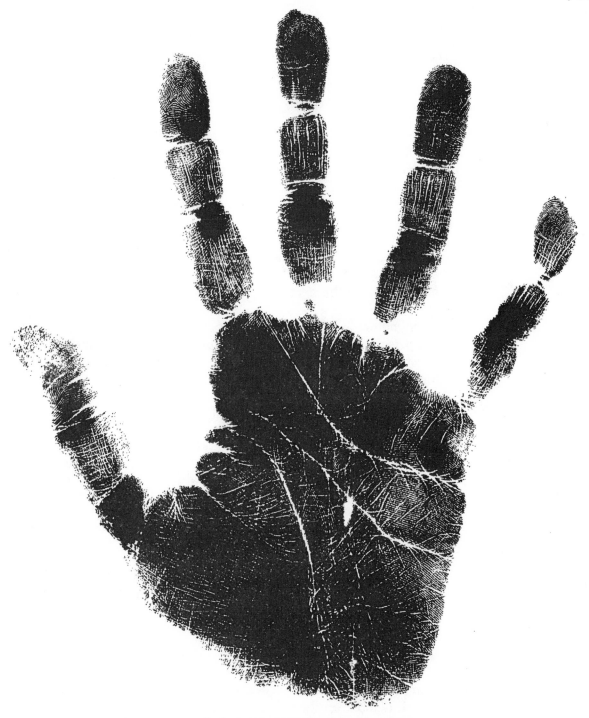

In the hand of Martine Getty, the heart line tends toward Jupiter with a branch toward the mount of Saturn. The mounts of Jupiter and Luna are strongest in her hand, indicating that money, travel and creativity will powerfully affect her life.

fade out halfway across the palm, meaning this person is cautious about involvement in general, whether with individuals or with humanity. She needs distance in her emotional relationships, and will always hold people more or less at arm's length. This doesn't mean she's incapable of giving affection; if the line is deep she's a great cuddler. She just needs plenty of time and space to herself.

Sometimes you will see a person whose heart line ends somewhere in the middle of the hand, signifying, as mentioned above, that she is a bit diffident about involvement. Then, apparently from nowhere, you might see a new branch of the heart line which either connects with or hangs there above the end point of the original heart line, and which ends in this space between Jupiter and Saturn. (It's less complicated than it sounds.) This is very good. It means that through some relationship or through increased self-knowledge our subject has moved away from that "don't bother me" attitude and has developed a capacity to be close to and commit herself to another human. The stronger this new branch is, the stronger is the new capacity for love.

All these endings are affected by the condition of the line itself. For example, if the person's line is weak and broken but ends in Jupiter, she may want to be ambitious and passionate but lacks the spirit to really pull it off. If the line is:

clear and deep, she is secure, loving and affectionate in love.

weak or chained, she is insecure and always seeking fulfillment. Intermittent dark spots on a chained heart line imply that the person broods about the inconstancy of love and goes through periods of depression.

strong and ends in three branches at the end, one going up into Jupiter or Saturn, one going all the way across the hand, and one ending halfway across, many forms of emotional expression are possible for her. She may be humanitarian one day, aloof the next, and a model parent or spouse the day after that. Or she could show all three sides within an hour. If her loved ones can cope with her changeability, this person can be quite intriguing.

High Hearted?

After you've looked at the direction and the form of the heart line, note whether it is high up on the palm, relatively close to the fingers, or down closer to the head line. If it doesn't strike you as exceptionally high or low, don't worry about it; it's probably average. If it is high, it implies that the person is very touchy and subjective. She needs constant reassurance from

We see again how the universe naturally compensates weaknesses with strengths. The low-set and tasseled heart line signifies an objective and untrusting emotional life. However, the Girdle of Venus travels up to the space between Jupiter and Saturn, showing that through cultivating sensitivity for people in general, this woman is healing her own heart.

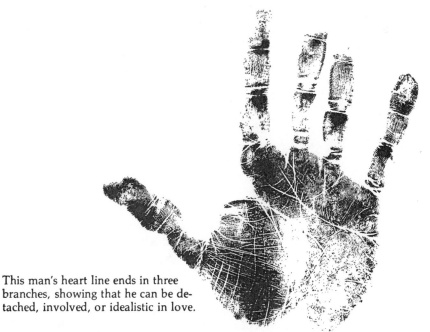

This man's heart line ends in three branches, showing that he can be detached, involved, or idealistic in love.

those close to her: "Do you really like it, honey?" If the heart line stretches down across the area of the head line, the intellect is strongly influencing this person's emotional life. That is, she tends to be rather calculating or objective about affairs of the heart. Ask her to run off with you to the Casbah and she'll tell you there are too many insects.

Head Lines

Just as a long life line does not necessarily mean a Methuselan life, so a long head line does not guarantee a high I.Q. The *shape* of the head line tells you the way this person's mind habitually works—whether she is naturally analytical, imaginative or a little nutty. The *form* of the line (deep, chained, etc.) tells you her psychological disposition—whether she thinks clearly and directly, or can't hold a thought for five seconds. It can also show some mental disturbances such as depression and occasionally points to physical problems of the brain and head. The *length* of the line tells you about the person's mental flexibility. So, you are looking at shape, form and length. If the line:

runs straight across the hand, it reflects an analytical, extremely incisive mind. Sometimes these people are so insightful that even they don't want to know all the things they know.

forks into sections, one straight and one sloped downward, you can be sure that she has a balanced capacity to see both sides of a situation. She can use her intellect when necessary or sprinkle in a little imagination when the moment is right.

bends slightly toward Luna, she has a clever and versatile imagination.

angles sharply toward Luna, she has an irrepressible imagination that can sometimes border on mental illness unless tempered or held in check by some other aspect of her life.

angles severely down and exactly parallels the life line, it is the sign of a very creative writer or composer. The angling head line retains its meaning of potential insanity and powerful imagination; however, when it is keyed in to the life line, this wild energy can be harnessed and put to work in creative endeavors.

Occasionally you'll see a square enclosing the farthest reaches of an angling head line. This means that any potential insanity has been controlled by some benevolent influence in the person's life, whether within herself or through a friend, or possibly through some spiritual influence.

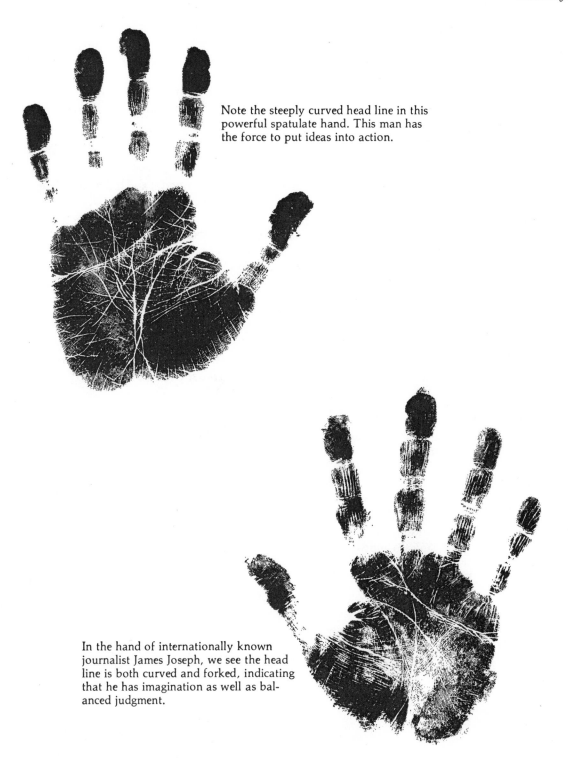

Note the steeply curved head line in this powerful spatulate hand. This man has the force to put ideas into action.

In the hand of internationally known journalist James Joseph, we see the head line is both curved and forked, indicating that he has imagination as well as balanced judgment.

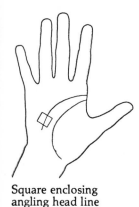

Square enclosing
angling head line

Next, as with the other lines, examine the overall condition of the head line, and temper your conclusions about the general mental state of the person with your feeling about the quality of energy shown on the line itself. If the form of the line is:

> *clear and deep,* you are hand in hand with a clear thinker. If a straight line is clear, the person comes to rational conclusions smoothly and quickly. If a person has a curved clear head line, she uses imagination freely without constraint.

> *faint or chained,* the person is hazy-minded, moody, and has a hard time following any thought through to a conclusion.

> *wavering,* she can come to a reasonable conclusion, but can't seem to do it in a reasonable way. She has to amble back and forth between the obvious and the obscure until the obvious hits her in the face.

The Long, the Short, and the Separate

A long line indicates a flexible, versatile mind. If the line is quite long but doesn't reach all the way across the hand, the subject has many diverse interests; if the entire line or mounts are weak, she may become a professional dilettante, unable to master anything.

Head line cutting
across hand

> *If the line cuts clear across the hand,* this person has more insight than most people care to have. When the hand is cut in two by a horizontal line, energy flow between the two halves of the hand is disrupted. So what, you might ask. It means that her vision cuts her in two. From an intellectual standpoint, this makes her bitingly analytical and scathingly insightful. From an emotional standpoint, who wants to know? Only exceptionally sturdy people are really interested in truth. From an energy standpoint, the more primal energies from the mounts of Venus and Luna are impeded as they try to seep into the active parts of the hand.

For example, a few years ago I read the hand of a poet. His right hand showed the curved line one would expect from a creative writer. His left hand had this crosscut line. I told him the interpretation of this combination of lines, and he told me a little more about his background. He had been a physicist, trying to bite down on the hard facts of reality. The more scientific he tried to be, the more he tore apart his emotional relationships, and the more miserable he became. Gradually, he followed an interest in creative writing and left the broken transistors behind.

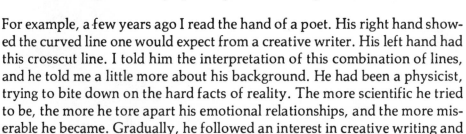

Short head line

> *A short line* indicates fixity of purpose, which sometimes borders on narrow-minded obsession. People who are absolutely brilliant at *one* thing, like backgammon, often have clear stubby head lines. If you really

The space between the head and life lines of songwriter F. Scott Newberry shows that he is impulsive and independent; this tendency is mitigated by the clarity of the lines and the fork in his head line. The heart line shows a deep capacity for affection.

Very young people often have very strong lines. In 20-month-old Fay Elanor Ellwood, a strong will is already shown by the hyper-extended thumb and the space between head and life lines, and balanced emotion is shown by the placement of the heart line.

want to get a point across to people with lines like this, find out what their subject is and explain everything in terms of that.

If the head line is joined to the life line for more than a quarter inch or so, the person was closely tied to her family in early life, and continues to be influenced by this as an adult. The longer the two lines run together, the longer the period of family dependence lasted. Such people tend to be quite cautious about change and new situations.

This timidity can be lessened by several factors, such as a strong thumb or a widely arching life line. Either of these implies that the person obeyed her parents for a while, but turned out to be too ornery to stick around.

If there's a narrow space between the life and head lines, the person is naturally independent and has been from the start. Such people are usually free-spirited and self-motivated. Combine this with a long, well-formed thumb and maybe a few spatulate fingertips, and you've got a sure winner.

If there's a wide space between head and life, this subject is too impetuous for her own good. Such people are always planning their assault on the Himalayas but can't seem to get to the grocery store. Rash decisions and mindless willfulness make these people the ones who have great ideas that never get off the ground.

The Simian Line

If the head line and the heart line merge into one line that cuts across the palm, the combination is called the simian line. It received this flattering name because monkeys often exhibit the same pattern. Interpretations of the simian line vary, and none of them are too complimentary. Fred Gettings, the English palmist, claims that simianites are likely to be either criminals or religious fanatics. He says these types have in common a strong inner tension that makes them seek extreme solutions to their life problems.

My explanation is a bit more general; I see this line as representing an incapacity to distinguish clearly between the heart and the mind. This does lead to tremendous confusion and inner struggle, and can make a person cold-blooded in situations that call for warmth and fill her with silly romanticism in straightforward business situations. Sometimes the effects of this line are mitigated by a Girdle of Venus, which increases the person's sensitivity in emotional matters, but if the sensitivity becomes too strong, even that can become a problem.

Have a little sympathy for people with this line. The mind and heart are naturally polarized so that they balance each other; putting them together on the same line is like mixing baking soda and vinegar.

Prepare to Meet Your Fate Line

The fate line does not represent the rubber stamp of fate; rather it is the path to achievement. Like all lines, it represents a person's capacities, and also indicates her attitudes towards success. A strong fate line indicates a secure career and home. A nonexistent fate line indicates that conventional forms of security are not important, or that the person does not know what she likes to do. Without a fate line, one may have a vigorous and interesting life, but she'll never have a sense of "path" or true vocation. Since ambition and achievement are usually related, this line is also a gauge of the person's drive for success.

As with all other main lines, the general tone of the fate or degree of security can be judged by the quality of the line itself, and the marks have their usual meanings. I have arbitrarily decided that the "origins" of the line will be closer to the wrist and the "endings" will be closer to the fingers.

Origins:

Fate line between
Venus and Luna

If it springs from the life line, it implies success arising from one's own efforts. Successful independent business people often have this line, particularly if the hands are square. Square hands, if you recall, indicate a talent for practical thought.

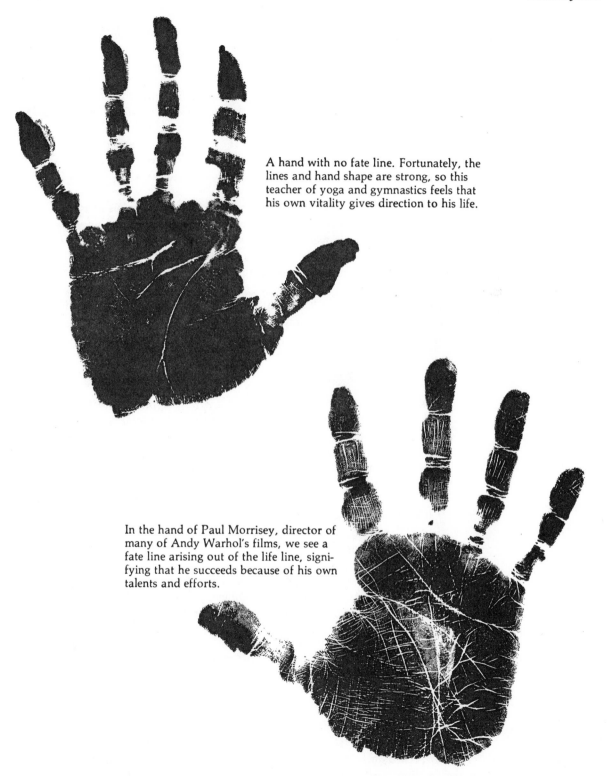

A hand with no fate line. Fortunately, the lines and hand shape are strong, so this teacher of yoga and gymnastics feels that his own vitality gives direction to his life.

In the hand of Paul Morrisey, director of many of Andy Warhol's films, we see a fate line arising out of the life line, signifying that he succeeds because of his own talents and efforts.

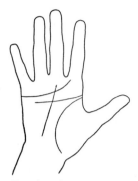

Fate line leaning
into Luna

If it rises from the middle of the palm between Venus and Luna, the person can expect solid good luck resulting from an excellent balance between work for herself and help from others.

If it leans into Luna, success will be based on luck and the assistance of other people. It also indicates that the person's work will be associated with helping others. Intuition will be used in nearly all of the person's business dealings. Depending on the shape of the hand and the shape of the head line, this line can belong to groups as diverse as lawyers, nurses, teachers, psychologists, and housewives.

If it extends deep into Luna, the career will be based in some spiritual or psychic practices. I have seen this line on the hands of professional psychics and healers as well as on the hands of people in other fields who knew that they often had flashes of knowledge about the past or future of people they met, or had precognitive dreams.

If the line begins at the head line, the person finds her career in midlife. If you see this mark on a floundering youngster, assure her that she'll find her way eventually.

Endings:

Fate line ending
deep in Luna

If the line ends deep in the mount of Jupiter, the person will have a career in the public eye. This can mean work in politics, music, theater, or anything that implies fame as a direct result of professional work or personal magnetism. If the line ends in a star on Jupiter, she is destined for immense fame and fortune. (True stars are as rare on hands as they are in life.)

If it ends deep in the mount of Saturn, she can look forward to secure success throughout life. This line marks the people who are most likely to get what they want from their lives.

If it ends between Saturn and Apollo, her career will relate to some aspect of the arts which requires technical expertise; architects, illustrators, sound engineers and other artistically-oriented types may have this line.

Marriages and Kids

Fate line ending
in Jupiter

Look for the little lines that describe the big event on the Mercury finger side of the hand. If there are any, they'll be the little horizontal lines above the mount of Luna near the heart line. Traditionally, each line represents a marriage or serious affair. However, having seen several people who have two marriage lines and no marriages, or no marriage lines and several marriages,

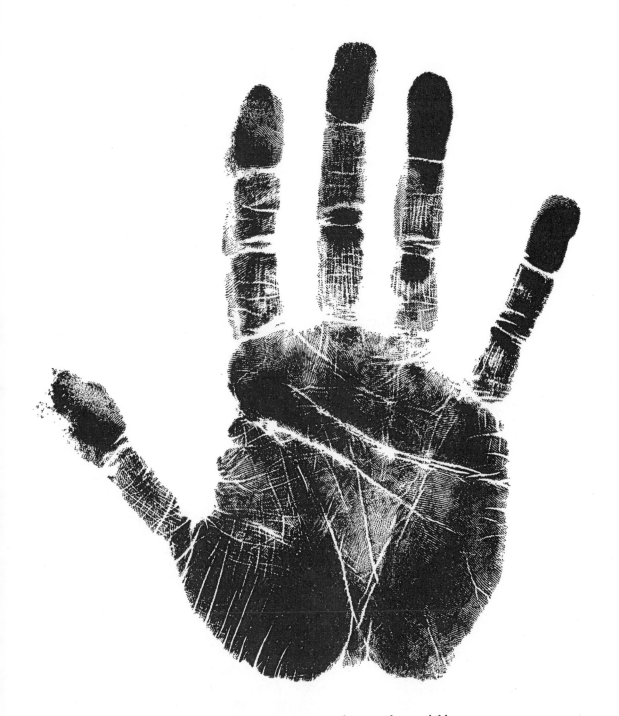

Two strong marriage lines, with two child lines coming from each marriage, are evident in this young man's hand.

I've concluded that each marriage line marks a *potential* marriage. If you meet someone whose hand is line-free along the side, she will probably not marry at all, and her commitments to *any* marriage will be limited. If a person has no distinct marriage lines but has many small horizontal lines on the side of the hand, she is like a bee who takes from many flowers. Be discreet if her mate is listening!

By marriage, I mean a spiritual, physical and emotional alliance. Your hand doesn't know anything about certificates and ceremonies. As with all lines, these lines represent propensities rather than certainties, and have been known, like marriages, to change.

The length of the marriage is related to the length of the marriage line, but it also represents the intensity of the person's desire to keep the marriage alive. It also shows changes within the marriage. For example, a couple once came to me for readings. Both were in their mid-fifties, and they had been married twenty-five years. The man, Jerry, was thinking of selling his successful business so that he could devote more time to his true interests, sailing and carpentry. Marian wanted to take art lessons and spend less time at home, but she was afraid to upset Jerry. Have you heard this story before?

Much of the conflict in the marriage arose from Jerry's rigid ideas about his own role and his expectations of Marian to be the ultimate homemaker. His stiff Saturn finger and heart line ending in Saturn revealed that his ideas of right and wrong were inflexible, and he was unreasonably idealistic in his expectations of his loved ones. He had only one long, deep marriage line which was divided into two sections. About halfway across the line there was a weakening, and then a brief break. The same line picked up again just after the break and continued nearly to the mount of Mercury on the front of the palm. Based on this, I told them they were on the verge of a major change in their relationship, but that if each of them were willing to give up a little security and some of the rigidity preventing both of them from doing what they enjoyed, the marriage would begin again after a brief separation.

Remember that the marriage line you are reading belongs to only one of the couple. Thus, one partner might be devoted to the marriage while the other is running around. I once read for a couple who lived like this. Curt, who had married a woman several years his elder, had only one long, deep and clear marriage line. When he met Marie, he felt he had met the love of his life. Although he had several affairs on the side, he needed to know that Marie was there for him when he came home, and he never really wanted to leave the wife who had become for him the embodiment of womanhood. His wife is more flighty. With two marriages behind her and a heart line roaming deep into Jupiter, she was looking out for Number One. With Curt's income, Marie could live very well. She continued to shop around while remaining enough of an embodiment of womanhood (and being home often enough) that he never divorced her. Curt's need for Marie is so strong that there is almost nothing she can do to break his affection for her. This is evident from the fact that his line is strong while her marriage lines are many and weak, and also from the fact that he hasn't left her.

Beware the Role of Marriage Counselor

Occasionally a couple will come to you and ask you to judge their compatibility. If they have to ask a palmist whether they get along, something's already fishy, but play dumb in the beginning. Rather than look for good or bad lines in each individual, look for a balance of mutual needs. If one person is fiery and the other cool, their chances for staying together are good. They may just need to talk to each other more often. If they are equally frenetic, they may drive each other nuts, and if they are equally passive, they may have trouble getting anything started, even an interesting argument. You don't have to be a palm reader to know this. However, you might be able to clarify the relationship to the would-be lovebirds by looking at their hands.

You can see each individual's attitudes and needs from the heart line, but you'll have to look to the marriage lines of both partners to see how well the match is actually working. Most of your comments about a marriage or a partner should be phrased positively in terms of the possibility for being happy, especially if both partners are listening. However, if you have a very strong intuitive feeling that the person for whom you are reading is being hurt physically or emotionally by the relationship, make your criticism stronger.

If you see, for example, that one partner is naturally ebullient—having those voluptuous red mounds on the *nondominant hand*, and you find on the *dominant hand* that much of this energy has been suppressed into pale, weak mounts and lines, you can conclude that this person's natural temperament is being repressed by her environment. Point out that a marriage is supposedly a combination of two lives, and it's not fair if one person is being squelched. They might not have looked at it this way before.

Bear in mind, however, that some people love to suffer. They're familiar with it, and if you tell them to change it, they will simply think you are wrong and continue on their not so merry way. If you sense that a woman's nasty husband is the man she loves to hate, keep your helpful suggestions to yourself. We palmists are not psychotherapists, and should not try to be. Learn from the experiences of the many policemen who are injured every year while trying to break up domestic fights; they may not like each other, but if you criticize their unhappiness, they'll *hate you.*

Color of the Lines

In addition to the length and strength of the line, the color of the skin around the lines as well as any marks or dark spots on the lines tell you a great deal, especially about marriage lines and heart lines. Your intuition will be extremely helpful as you identify and expand on the various possibilities.

White puffy areas around the line indicate uncried tears. Puffy areas on any line on the palm indicate that the person has not yet "processed" the pain associated with that area of her life. If the puffiness extends the length of a marriage line, then the marriage is such a source of misery that she can no longer remember whatever possessed her to get married. If there is a brief puffy period, then there is now, or has been in the recent past, a period of heartache from which the person has not yet recovered. Whenever you see this sign, remind the subject gently that the only way to get rid of psychological pain is to bring it out into the open and experience it, and that holding it in will only make her sick. Also, if the pain is caused by a relationship, the person is not being fair to her partner if she never speaks up. Suggest that she ask herself clearly what the problem is and, after clarifying it to herself through reflection or talking to a close friend, she talk it over with her partner and see if they can come to a better understanding. If a better understanding is impossible or if, for example, the spouse is already dead or has abandoned the person who has this puffy area, remind her that she'll be better off if she cries herself out now, and then moves on to happier possibilities. If there are other people listening, simply tell the person that you could be more specific if you met in private. Then be available to meet in private. Otherwise you can be legitimately accused of being a tease.

Redness in or around the line is a sign of passion and often implies active anger. However, make sure your client doesn't just have dishpan hands. The redness should appear on some specific part of the line in order to rate as a bona fide message. If the line is red, at least the person is fighting out her problems instead of suffering silently.

Darkness on the line is difficult to describe, and is something you will develop a feel for as you read more hands. It usually indicates depression, sullenness, resentment, etc., but it can also imply inactivity or an inability to be involved in a relationship at that moment due to forces beyond the individual's control.

When trying to read subtle variations in color or marks on minor lines, breathing deeply and staying open to the voice of your intuition are more helpful than any textbook.

Children

Another popular question! The small vertical lines bouncing out of each marriage line are traditionally associated with children. However, like children, these lines are not always reliable. Miscarriages and abortions

Larry Grobel Well-known journalist and
writer. Although he is a creative writer in
his own right, he is best known for his
interviews in Playboy Magazine with
Marlon Brando, Barbra Streisand, Dolly
Parton, Steve Martin, Al Pacino, and
other superstars.

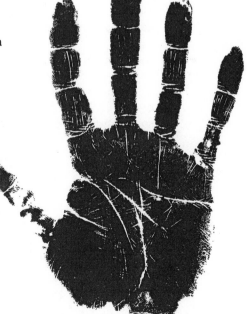

The Apollo line ends above the heart line,
indicating that this woman loves the arts,
although she is not a professional artist.

sometimes show up as weak or short child lines and sometimes people who want to have children never get around to actually giving birth. For every person with two child lines who has no kids, I'm convinced that somebody with two child lines had quadruplets. One way or another, it all balances out.

The Line of Apollo

The line of Apollo is also known as the line of the Sun, the secondary life line or the secondary fate line. But a rose is a rose is a rose. Not everyone has this line, and not everyone misses it. It signifies an additional source of life energy, particularly the energy of the arts. This line strengthens the whole hand, but remember that the influence of the major lines is always greater than that of a secondary line. The most deeply etched Apollo cannot overcome the influence of fuzzy life or head lines.

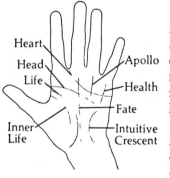

If the line begins on the mount of Apollo and washes out above the heart line, this extra vigor takes the form of a general artistic sensibility and, if combined with a decent thumb, head line and fate line, corroborates the fact that the person is likely to succeed at anything she attempts. Remember that the basic temperament was determined in pages past under hand shape and major lines.

If the line of Apollo extends below the head line, this person seriously considers herself an artist. She will create. The type of creation and the degree of success are again dependent on the shape of the hands and the overall condition of the lines. If there are several lines of Apollo, the person has artistic talent in several areas.

The Health Line vs. The Intuitive Crescent

Most people don't have either of them, but for those who do, here's the story: The health line, also called the line of Liver, runs from just below the Mercury finger to various spots on the life or fate lines. The Intuitive Crescent arcs up from the mount of Luna toward the Mercury finger. Although they sometimes occupy the same territory, they are not the same. Some authors claim that the presence of the health line signals increased health, and others claim that it heralds sickness; This is very helpful to newcomers in the field. My feeling is that health is best gauged by color, texture, temperature, humidity, and degree of vitality in a hand rather than by examining the health line. Experience tells me that if the health line looks red and inflamed, toxins are actively polluting the body. If it is clear, it's a sign of well-toned vital organs. Use the marks listed in Chapter 5 for most medical palmistry, but consider the condition of the health line as a reflector of the person's ability to detoxify himself. Most important, remember that its presence is not that important.

The Intuitive Crescent appears lower on the hand than the health line and is (surprise!) crescent-shaped rather than straight. It represents a visceral, intuitive insight which borders on the instinctual. On an otherwise simple or elementary hand, it shows a strong impulse toward responding from the gut rather than the head or heart. Thus, it is not always a positive sign. You might have an impulse to punch someone in the face, but you don't necessarily act that impulse out, do you? One who does might have an Intuitive Crescent, a coarse powerful thumb, and a Himalayan mount of Venus. In gentler hands the Intuitive Crescent shows a strong gut intuition which is tempered by the softer aspects of the hand.

Lines of Influence

Lines of influence are lines that have no specific name. They appear in different forms on each palm. Some palms have only the three or four major lines, while others are like a street map of Manhattan. Like all lines, they are rivers, carrying energy from one part of the palm to another. It is in reading the lines of influence that you will really test the fine tuning of your palm-reading ability, since you must use your knowledge of the parts of the palm from which the energy is traveling and to which it is going in order to interpret what each line of influence means.

In general, vertical or gently sloping lines are simple messenger lines, carrying "telegrams" of energy all around the palm; for example, if you see a heart line with many little offshoots streaming down toward the head line, there is strong interaction between the intellect and the heart. If these lines originate more from the head line, then the intellect is trying to dominate that tender heart. If the order is reversed, then the heart is trying to cloud what might be simple intellectual or commonsense issues with a lot of silly romanticism. If the palm is splattered with so many small lines of influence that you can barely pick out the main line, the person is high-strung and overflowing with nervous electrical energy. You needn't interpret each one of these lines.

Now you have covered everything from the major to the minor leagues. Life line, head line, and fate line have given you basic information about physical vitality, major life events, emotional attitudes and the degree and type of ambition that keeps the person ticking. Not only that, you have looked for Apollo lines, health lines, marriage lines, baby lines, and you have used your astonishing palmistic prowess to interpret the nameless lines of influence. Your friends are agog.

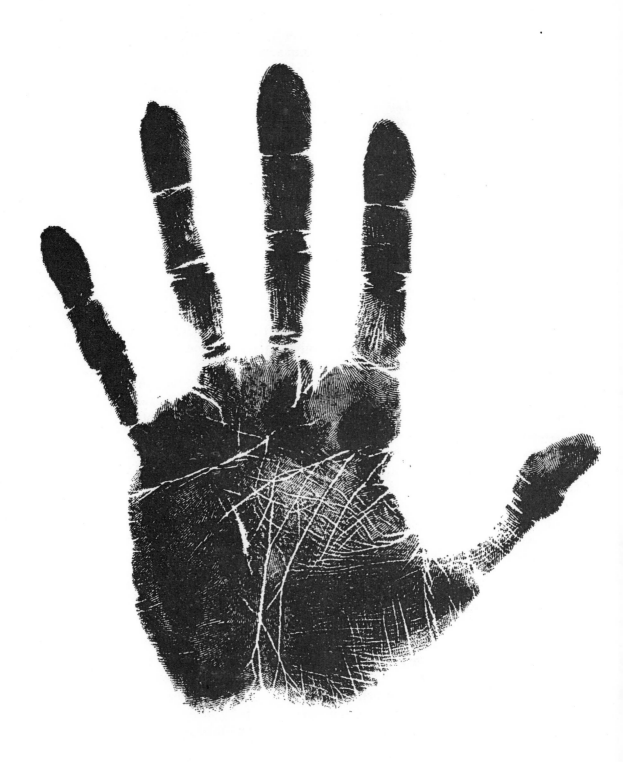

Guess Whose

Look at the hand on the left. You can see it is basically square, implying that this person is basically practical and rational. Looking at the quadrants, you see that the Jupiter and Saturn fingers are both longer than the Apollo and Mercury fingers, and that the mount of Venus is thicker than the mount of Luna. Also, the mount of Jupiter is the thickest of any of the finger-related mounts. From this you can conclude that this person is far more interested in activities of the outer world than of the inner mind.

Now let's look at the lines. The life line seems to begin the course it follows for most of the hand about 3/4" into the hand, under the mount of Jupiter. Before that time, there is a strong period very early in the life, and then in the middle teens, you can see a small branch rising from the life line and creating an island. This could mean a short trip which radically diminishes the person's life energy for a time, or forces his natural temperament to go underground, or a period in which the person is struggling to find his own direction. This island shows a brief break just at its center. This means that the person was very ill or that his life nearly stopped at that point in his mid-teens. Gradually, the life line picks up again, and after a few more years of uncertainty, the main path of his life begins in his early to mid-20s. Throughout this period he has a very strong inner life line, implying a reserve of energy which he calls on in times of stress.

The head line is tied in to the problems in the life line until the mid-20s, when the person breaks free of the influence of the island on the life line, and begins to use his mind more clearly. The line is slightly curved, implying that he has a creative imagination which he can use, but which will not drive him insane. The heart line is somewhat chained, implying that the person has difficulty trusting the ones he loves. However, it is not as chained as many other hands, so we can assume he is willing to give his loved ones a chance to prove themselves worthy of his affection.

The heart line ends in three branches, one to the space between Jupiter and Saturn, one to the center of the mount of Jupiter, and one which descends to the head line. This means that the person varies between being affectionately loving (space between Jupiter and Saturn), being aloof and distant (heart line dangling in the middle of the hand), and responding intellectually rather than emotionally in his love relationships (influence from the head line on the heart).

The fate line arises from the life line, which means that this man wants to make a name for himself without being too dependent on the help of others. He is in his early 20s now; the end of the line may change as he gets older. If you look closely, you can see a small branch tying together the end of the existing fate line with the branch of the heart line, which ends between Jupiter and Saturn. If this branch becomes stronger, it would imply that the person's career is related to activities in the public eye, but that he himself will not be a performer.

Since the mounts of Jupiter and Venus are particularly strong, we know that money, power and physical comforts are extremely important to this individual.

Now look for a moment at the nondominant (left) hand. Basically, the lines are similar, but note these differences: The life line angles more acutely toward Luna. The fate line is further separated from the life line. Also, there is a branch of the heart line which actually ends on Saturn, and which could be seen as the beginning of a Girdle of Venus. The other half of the girdle is the line angling down between Apollo and Mercury. The nondominant hand, as you recall, shows the inner life or innate capacities of the person. Judging by this hand, one would think that this man travels the world constantly, and is fairly dependent on others for his means of support. The heart line branch to Saturn indicates he is quite idealistic about love, and the beginning Girdle of Venus shows he is exceptionally sensitive. The idealism is probably lurking inside him still, but the changes in the life and fate line from the dominant to the nondominant hand indicate that he has changed the direction of the life he was born into.

This is the palm print of John Paul Getty III, who was kidnapped from his home in Rome in his mid-teens and who suffered at the hands of his kidnappers until his family paid an enormous ransom. Although he could have entered his family's business empire, he wants to make a career for himself in the film business, not as an actor but as a director or producer. His hands show the intensity of his urge to live, and the importance of using his imagination to make something which is a physical reflection of the world in which he lives.

5

Medical Palmistry

You can read health conditions from the hands just as accurately as you read life situations. Although diagnosis through the hands should not be substituted for a trip to the doctor, it can clue you in to potential health problems before they turn into full-fledged diseases. There are two ways of looking at disease—sickness seen as an unavoidable enemy to be combated and suppressed, or seen as a preventable, sometimes helpful sign that energies in the body are out of balance. American and European doctors have traditionally followed the "unavoidable enemy" approach, which is why most of us have been trained to think sickness is something that strikes suddenly, and our bodies can be "fixed" if we add the right chemicals or cut out the troublesome part. Oriental medicine has historically been more concerned with prevention and treating the entire body even when only one part is sick, on the assumption that, since the whole body is connected, the problems of one part affect the well-being of all parts. According to this line of reasoning, a potential illness shows itself in subtle ways all over the body long before the most serious symptoms appear. Traditional doctors share this belief to some degree, but not to the point that they will diagnose and *treat* disease before it becomes a major problem.

Before exploring the patterns of abnormal skin ridges and hands in disease, a brief note about statistics is in order. Statistics is a mathematical tool used to determine what the odds are that a certain event will happen by chance. For example, if you flip a coin, the odds that it will come up heads

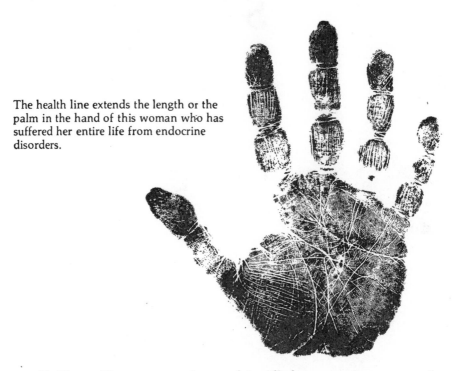

The health line extends the length or the palm in the hand of this woman who has suffered her entire life from endocrine disorders.

are 50–50, or 50 percent, or 1 out of 2. All those terms are ways of saying that if you flip that coin 100 times, it will most likely come up heads 50 times and tails 50 times; however, if heads turns up 75 or 85 times, some other factor is coming into play. The odds against this happening by chance alone are diminishing rapidly, and the odds that something else is causing it to happen are increasing proportionately. The term "statistically significant" means that the odds against the event happening the number of times it happened are so great that it cannot have happened by chance alone. For example, if you toss a coin 100 times and get heads 100 times, an objective observer would suppose that you either have a two-headed coin or you are a budding Uri Geller.

Differences which appear to be significant over a small number of trials often turn out to be insignificant over a large number of trials. If you flip a coin 25 times and get 25 heads, don't call Johnny Carson's talent coordinator right away. At the end of 100 or 1,000 throws you'll probably end up 50-50. This raises an important point about accepting any scientific research as definite proof of the conclusions the researcher is presenting. Good research projects work by isolating variables, deciding on a specific counting or judging technique, and using a large enough number of cases to be sure their results are not only the result of chance. The more studies which support a conclusion, the more likely it is that the conclusion is true.

As a student of medical palmistry, you need to know this for two reasons: First, it will help you evaluate the information in this chapter. Dermatoglyphic research on schizophrenia and genetic aberrations have been confirmed by a variety of researchers in studies of thousands of people. Unfortunately, these researchers frequently used different techniques—some studied finger lengths, others looked for breaks in the ridges on the palm. The result is that all agree schizophrenia can be seen in the hand but few agree on exactly what makes a schizophrenic's hand different. In other cases, one or two studies of a small number of people produced startling results. Until studies on many more people are completed, these results should be seen as interesting possibilities rather than definite proofs.

More important to your everyday practice of medical palmistry is this: In using these results to gauge illness, you are dealing with odds, not certainties. Until you have supporting evidence from other sources, including other marks on the hands, be skeptical. Use medical palmistry to increase your friends' awareness of their own bodies and their capacity to improve their own health, not to frighten them or to show them how much you know.

Goethe once said, "We see what we look for, we look for what we know." Most doctors don't look closely at the hands during a clinical examination because they think the ridges on the skin are there only to help keep things from slipping out of our hands and the creases are the result of flexing the hands. (Lines are always referred to as "flexion creases" in medical literature.) The first belief is only partly true, since there would be no need for every fingerprint to be unique if the only function of ridged skin was to help us keep our grip; the second is patently false, since our palmar creases are fully formed before the fourth month of prenatal life.

You'll be looking at palms more closely than most doctors, and there will be times when you feel sure about a diagnosis. However, unless you are a licensed physician, DO NOT DIAGNOSE! You can mention that there's an irregularity somewhere and suggest a complete physical checkup, but please, don't try to practice medicine without a license. Here you see the results of a computerized bibliographic search which turned up over two hundred articles in recognized medical journals concerning the diagnostic uses of observing the lines, fingerprints and shapes of the hands. The articles came from England, the United States, France, Italy, Germany, Japan, Poland and Russia. Subjects ranged from a comparison of modern man's fingerprints with prints found on Stone Age pottery (the basic patterns and lines are the same) to a number of articles correlating specific marks on the hands with mental illness. Some of these studies produced statistically significant results; others did not.

In addition to the research articles, references for this chapter include Dr. T. J. Berry's medical text, *The Hand as a Mirror of Systemic Disease; A Doctor's Guide to Better Health Through Palmistry* by Eugene Scheimann, M.D.; and *The Human Hand* by Dr. Charlotte Wolff. All the research indicates that progress reports on our health are constantly being given out through signs in our hands. Learn to read them and how to adjust your diet and lifestyle to improve them, and you'll have one more tool to help you

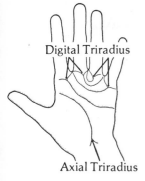

Digital Triradius

Axial Triradius

Triradius

Tented arch

Loop

stay happy and healthy. (Or at least healthy, which is a step in the right direction.)

There are two distinctively different aspects of hands that we need to examine for medical palmistry: The marks which are unchangeable structural defects in the person's genetic or physical makeup, and the marks which show temporary, correctable imbalances.

Accepting the Unchangeable

From these unchangeable aspects of the hands you can tell a person's predispositions to certain forms of mental illness or retardation, congenital heart disease and behavioral problems such as hyperkinesis in children or obsessive tendencies in adults. The only parts of the hands which can never change spontaneously are the skin ridges on the fingers and palms and the length and angle of insertion of the fingers. Ridge patterns on the palms (and the soles of the feet) are called "dermatoglyphics," which literally means "skin carvings."

Dermatoglyphics run in nearly parallel rows all over the hands, tracing tented arches, loops in two directions, and whorls in patterns unique to every human being. Even the hands of identical twins are slightly different, having about the same degree of variation as that between the right and left hands of most individuals. Finger and hand prints have intrigued human beings for generations; cave men plastered their prints on the walls of their living rooms and early Sanskrit scholars coined a word for "fingerprints." However, the first academic mention of dermatoglyphs in European medical history came in 1684. After that there were a few desultory mentions of the glyphs in anatomy textbooks until the next breakthrough with the work of Galton in the late nineteenth century.

It was Galton who sifted through reams of fingerprints and culled out the basic patterns according to which we still classify those graceful tracings on our hands. The originator of modern dermatoglyphics was Harold Cummins, who pioneered the use of fingerprints as a means of identification and as a tool in criminal investigation. Galton's classification system is based on the *triradius.* Wherever three ridge systems meet you have a triradius. Look at your own palm or at any print in this book and you'll see easily the four major triradii of a normal hand. Three of them are between the fingers just above the heart line—one between the index and third fingers, one between the third and fourth fingers, and one between the fourth and fifth fingers. The fourth and most important triradius is at the base of the palm, centrally located just above the wrist crease. It is called the *axial triradius.* In addition to these major triradii of the palm, there are triradii on nearly all the fingertips. Galton classified all fingerprint patterns according to the number of triradii on each fingertip. Tented *arches* have no triradii, *radial and ulnar*

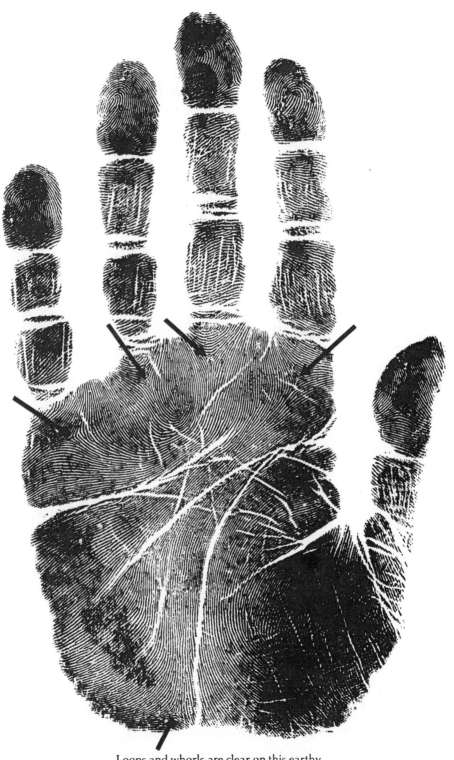

Loops and whorls are clear on this earthy hand. (Arrows show the major triradii.)

Whorls

loops have one, and *whorls* have two or, rarely, three. Radial loops point toward the thumb and ulnar loops point toward the fifth finger.

Loops are the most common pattern on normal hands, although it is common to find a few examples of other patterns as well. Whorls are most common to the thumb and fourth finger. Radial loops are most common on the index finger, and ulnar loops are most common on the fifth finger. Deviations from these normal patterns of distribution are among the signs that an individual was born unusual. Bear in mind that "unusual" or "abnormal" don't necessarily mean "bad"—Einstein was unusual and abnormal, although he was still a human being and his hands still looked roughly like everyone else's hands. Medical researchers Stough and Seeley note that abnormal dermatoglyphics are those in which there occur 1) an increased or decreased frequency of normal patterns; 2) unusual combinations of normal patterns; and 3) normal patterns in unusual places. You will never see a fingerprint that looks like a snowflake.

Since dermatoglyphics are formed so early in prenatal life, deformities in them must arise either because of a genetic malformation occurring during conception or as a result of a trauma to the fetus during early pregnancy. Such traumas might include the mother's taking methadone, thalidomide or other drugs, the mother's infection with German measles, or to other more subtle changes in the womb. The fact that studies show certain forms of mental illness, heart disease, breast cancer and alcoholism can be predicted with some accuracy supports the theory that certain people are innately disposed to developing these conditions, even under ideal environmental circumstances.

Most medical research on dermatoglyphics centers on genetic aberrations, German measles and schizophrenia. A few small studies have been done on breast cancer, alcoholism and leukemia, but the results have not been duplicated often enough to make the conclusions definite. The most frequent signs of genetic mishap, for example, Down's syndrome, are the simian line (single transverse crease), and the Sydney line (head line extending the full width of the hand). Researchers also look for broken ridge patterns, excess whorls and other unusual formations anywhere on the hand.

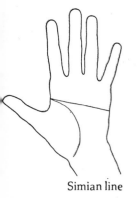

Simian line

The simian line was named by someone who never saw an ape up close. Small monkeys have hand lines similar to those of human beings and large apes have stray, confused lines all over the hands. It was once thought (probably by the same people who thought all simians had simian lines) that since the simian line looks like a monkey's hand it must be a regressive sign in human hands, and therefore there must be a stage in every embryo's development when it has a simian crease, too. This is what happens when you try to argue reasonably from a false assumption. The simian line appears on the palm as a simian line and stays that way throughout life. It is generally studied along with the Sydney line (named after the city), as both lines show an unusual genetic makeup.

As mentioned earlier, the simian crease is a classic symptom of Down's syndrome, since it and a very small thumb are the most prominent signs on the hands of people with that condition. (Down's syndrome is also known as mongolism.) Down's syndrome is caused by a foul-up in the initial bonding of the egg and the sperm in which the baby gets one too many chromosomes in each of his cells. However, not everyone who has a simian crease is an idiot. Mixed up, maybe, but not an idiot. Remember that the crease is only one of a whole group of symptoms of Down's syndrome, not the least of which is severe mental retardation. One important clue is that if someone *cares* whether or not he has a simian crease, he probably does not have Down's syndrome.

Even among non-mongoloids, the simian line is a bad sign. Premature, stillborn and congenitally damaged children are significantly more likely to have simian creases. In one study by R.J. Lerer, the incidence of lethal abnormalities was twice as high among children with simian creases than it was with children having non-simian palms. However, just over 50 percent of the simian crease children in this study appeared perfectly normal. As people with these creases grow up, those with extreme retardation or deformities either die or are institutionalized, so the odds are that any simian creases you run across will belong to the physically normal 50 percent. Nevertheless, adults with simian creases are somewhat more likely to have difficulty adjusting to society and to allow their interests to become obsessions.

Those with Sydney lines are two to three times more likely to have behavioral problems such as hyperactivity or speech and hearing problems when they are young. The editors of the magazine "Clinical Pediatrics" suggest that all physicians routinely examine their patients' hands and consider simian or Sydney lines as warning signs of hidden physical anomalies or latent behavioral problems. The Sydney line is more likely to show a tendency toward behavioral or adjustment problems, whereas the simian line is more likely to point to physical abnormalities. Retardation syndromes other than mongolism are often caused by chromosomal breakage; these often produce simian creases and deformations of the hands.

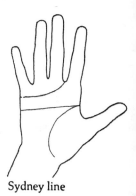

Sydney line

Schizophrenia

Schizophrenia is another illness frequently associated with abnormal dermatoglyphic patterns. Remember that schizophrenia is a form of insanity completely different from ordinary neurosis. The difference between neurosis and psychosis is like the difference between wishing you could be like Napoleon and believing you *are* Napoleon. Think of neurosis as the common cold of mental illness; psychosis is the collapsed lung. Neuroses can be overcome, and psychoses such as schizophrenia can improve, but there is no clear proof at this time that schizophrenia can be cured.

There are several types of schizophrenia, some of which can be treated more successfully than others. According to Dr. David Goodman, some types of madness definitely run in families; these are often the most difficult to treat. Other types arise spontaneously in individuals; they can sometimes be improved by drugs and therapies. The search for a cure to schizophrenia is like the search for a cure for cancer: Many diverse conditions are called by the same name, and researchers may come up every few months with "total cures" which turn out not to be effective in all cases. In general, catatonic schizophrenia (characterized by a zombie-like state) and hebephrenia (characterized by infantile regression) are the most difficult to treat.

In dermatoglyphic research, the most common finding is that schizophrenics have more broken or deformed ridges all over their hands, more random or accidental patterns around the triradii and on the mount of Venus, and more whorls on their fingertips. Several studies concluded that where there were more whorls there were correspondingly few ulnar loops. Ulnar loops are the most common and therefore the most normal marking on the fingertips, so a decreased frequency in abnormal hands is not surprising. The most seriously ill patients, the hebephrenics, had the most deviant ridges.

In *The Human Hand,* Dr. Charlotte Wolff reports that abnormal patterns of finger length usually point to severe psychological disorders. Normally the fingers follow the pattern 5-2-1-3-4, with 1 being the longest finger and 5 being the shortest (the thumb). Occasionally the fourth finger is as long as or slightly longer than the index finger in normal hands, but if the fourth finger is longer by far than the index or is nearly as long as the middle finger, the likelihood of severe psychological maladjustment increases. Dr. Wolff examined several catatonics in mental hospitals and found that all had fourth fingers as long as or longer than second fingers. I·have seen this phenomenon in the hands of several members of a strict religious cult which depends on unswerving loyalty to a patriarchal teacher and renunciation of the material world. From a palmistic viewpoint, the long fourth finger implies that the inner world is far more important than the outer world of social reality; the catatonic's retreat into silence and the devotee's incessant introspection certainly bear this out.

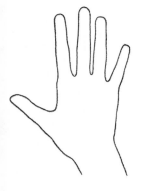

Normal finger
lengths

Dr. Wolff also reports that in a study of 110 schizophrenics, 85 percent had straight graceful fingers on sensitive hands. They differed from normal sensitive hands only in their ungainly mannerisms, in a noticeable atrophy of the muscles and in their extreme flexibility. She concluded that among subjects prone to schizophrenia, those with sensitive hands are most likely to become paranoids and those with abnormal finger length patterns are more likely to become catatonics.

Another symptom of latent schizophrenia is the exceptionally long, pointed fifth finger. A pinky extending to just above the crease between the middle and the top joints of the fourth finger would still be normal, signifying great talent in communication, providing that it appears on otherwise strong hands. Also, a long fifth finger on a long-fingered hand is not out of place. But if the pinky is disproportionately long and noticeably pointed, severe behavior problems and possible mental illness are indicated. This sign was reported by a variety of different researchers.

Although much research has been devoted to the relationship between dermatoglyphics and mental illness, little has been done to correlate the lines on the palm with mental distress. A sharply curving head line signifies an overactive imagination. If the line is deep and cuts sharply into the mount of Luna then the person can barely keep himself from tumbling headlong into the darkness of his own unconscious mind; in some cases this leads to mental illness. However, having an overactive fantasy life is not the same as being clinically insane. When you see a steep head line you know the person is sometimes too imaginative for his own good, since he must devote a lot of energy just to maintaining the facade of everyday life. According to Dr. Wolff, *broken* head lines are more common among mental retardates and habitual criminals. Until more research is done on the relationship between head lines and true psychosis, assume that sharply curved head lines indicate creative neurotics, broken head lines denote the stupid or periodically confused, and broken ridges, super pinkies, and abnormal finger lengths are the province of the truly certifiable.

Dr. Eugene Scheimann composed a checklist of signs which show a constitutional predisposition to mental illness. Since it is consistent with the medical research on the subject, I reprint it here. He lists:

1. Displaced axial triradius. (This can also be a sign of heart disease or genetic malformations, so it alone is not sufficient as a sign of mental illness.)
2. Whorls or loops on lines.
3. Increased composite (no specific form) markings on all fingers and on the mount of Venus.
4. Disassociated or ill-formed ridges known as "strings of pearls."

Also look for people conversing with invisible spirits, claiming to be Joan of Arc, refusing to speak for months at a stretch, and wetting the bed at age 45.

None of the studies which formed the background of this section offered explanation of why similar marks on the hands (the simian and Sydney lines) are related to dissimilar physical problems, ranging from prenatal exposure to German measles to having too much genetic material to having too little (i.e. broken) genetic material. The researchers were puzzled, but opted for staying puzzled rather than introduce the possibility that the creases on the hand mirror the mental and physical health of the person, regardless of whether the variations in health were caused by viral agents, genetic malformations or environmental influences. I do not know the exact mechanics of palmar line formation in the human fetus, but if it's true that specific aspects of the body/mind are mirrored in specific parts of the palm, then diverse agents which affect the same part of the body/mind will have the same effect on the part of the hand associated with that part of the body/mind. More specifically, if one accepts the premise that the head line represents the mental strength of an individual, then it is perfectly reasonable to presume the head line will be affected by any prenatal factor which influences the baby's mentality. This explains why viruses, drugs and broken genes can all have the same effect on the palm. If we go a step further we see that the tiny fetus, vibrating with expanding life, is vulnerable to the minutest changes in its world; thus the mother's mood and energy level might also affect the lines on the hands. The medical and the palmistic interpretations of the simian line are quite similar; perhaps one day their explanations will be similar, too.

Studies on Congenital Heart Disease

As mentioned earlier, several studies have linked unusual dermatoglyphic patterns with congenital heart disease. Drs. Takashina and Yorifuji reported that 64 percent of their male patients with congenital heart disease had axial triradii placed higher up toward the fingers or multiple axial triradii, compared to 17 percent of the normal control group. Those who had acquired heart disease or angina pectoris did not have these misplaced triradii. The subjects in this study were Japanese-Hawaiians. Odds are a billion to one against these results occurring by chance in a Japanese population. They are 6 million to one against it occurring in a white population and 1,640 to one against it occurring in a black population. If you spot an exceptionally high axial triradius, particularly in an Asian or a white person, look for corroborating signs of heart disease such as bluish nails, a break in the heart or life line, and clubbed fingertips. If you see any supporting signs, ask when the person's last complete physical exam was and whether he had an electrocardiogram taken at that time. If he hasn't had these checkups within the past year, suggest that he make an appointment to have them done. This would be particularly important if heart disease runs in the person's family.

The Thumb

Imagine life without your thumb and you'll see why a deformed or stunted thumb is frequently a sign of mental backwardness or behavioral abnormality. A fully functional thumb permits us to do all of our uniquely human manual activities—writing, fine craftsmanship, eating with utensils and so forth. It also permits us to grasp a three-dimensional object and sense all three dimensions at once, which contributes to the development of our entire sense of spatial relationship and size. Palmistic interpretations of the joints of the thumb were discussed in Chapter 2. In this section we'll cover the thumbs which clue you in to medical or psychiatric problems, namely, the simian thumb, the murderer's thumb and the degenerate thumb. Sound pretty appetizing, don't they?

"Simian thumb" refers to a thumb located well back toward the wrist at nearly a right angle to the hands. According to T. J. Berry, this is invariably a sign of a pathological mentality. Those are fighting words, but it is reputedly a 100 percent accurate sign of trouble. Don't contradict people with this type of thumb, don't believe a word they say, and back out the door as quickly as you can.

Murderer's thumbs are those which are broad and flat with a short wide nail, looking a bit as if they've been through a thumb press. Although they do have a cruel look, I've met several people who have them and all are decent, responsible and decisive individuals. Dr. Berry agrees that the term is unfair to the people who happen to inherit nasty-looking thumbs. They are included here because although they don't have a medical significance, people often think they do. Most likely, murderer's thumbs have been confused or grouped with clubbed, bulbous or degenerate thumbs and caused all this maligning of nice guys with broad flat thumbs. Clubbed, bulbous thumbs are signs of poor self-control and possible heart trouble.

"Murderer's thumb"

Just as a long, well-formed thumb is usually a sign of an intelligent and successful human being, so a short, defective thumb is usually a sign of a mentally defective or behaviorally deviant individual. The short, clubbed thumb on a hand where none of the other fingers are clubbed is likely a sign of cruelty and insensitivity, whereas a weak, stunted-looking thumb is more likely a sign of mental retardation.

Preventing the Preventable

Your body wants to be healthy. Long before you develop a cough or fever or something more serious, like a heart attack or a stroke, your body is fighting to maintain its equilibrium. Unfortunately, the biggest enemy in your body's fight for health might be you. If you don't feed your body what it needs, take it out for exercise and fresh air regularly and avoid debilitating mental habits like worrying, it won't be able to fight back when germs attack or parts start to break down. Your body is also *you*, not a car or bike that you can race into the ground and then trade in for a new one. During the long incubation period which precedes the obvious onset of all diseases your body gives off subtle signals of impending trouble. If you know that an illness is developing, you can act to prevent it from growing worse.

A common example is the feeling of coming down with the flu. Before you actually have to stay in bed, you feel run down, achy and out of sorts. If you recognize those as early warning signs, you can increase your fluid intake, get extra rest and imagine your body throwing off invading viruses. If you do these things early enough, you probably won't fall sick. If you don't respond to early signs, your body will weaken to the point that you have no alternative but to lie in bed and give it the rest it demands. Give your body what it needs when it needs it and it will cooperate by having the vitality you need to do all the things you like to do.

It's slightly misleading to refer to "your body" and "you" as though they were separate beings. Your body is an aspect of you, so when I say, "Your body is telling you such and such," it really means that one aspect of yourself is relaying information to another aspect of yourself about the overall condition of your entire being. It would be cumbersome to write all that out in every instance, so please understand that when I say, "Your body tells you," I mean "You tell yourself."

Your body warns you of developing imbalances in many ways. Obvious symptoms like a cough, pain or fever appear, as do less obvious signs such as changes in the texture of your nails or hair, spots in the iris of your eye and changes in your hands. In this section, we'll cover most of the early warning signals you can discover in your hands and the hands of your friends. By watching these signs you can increase your sensitivity to your own body and perhaps prevent yourself from getting sick. Remember, though, that knowing the warning signs won't help unless you respond to them by seeing a doctor and changing your diet, exercise or ways of coping with stress. We'll examine changes in the color, temperature, humidity and texture of the hands, variations in the shape and size of fingers, hand tremors, and finally, diagnosis through the nails.

Color Changes in the Hands

Ideally, hands should have a pinkish tone shining through the natural skin color. This implies a healthy, cheerful disposition. If the hands are not pink, the health and therefore the temperament are out of balance.

If hands are warm and have a bluish tone, there is a problem with the circulation. Depending on the degree of blueness and other signs on the palm, causes can range from heart disease, arteriosclerosis and certain blood diseases to Raynaud's syndrome, a circulatory ailment of young women in which their hands occasionally go blue and numb. It can also result from taking certain drugs. When you see warm blue hands, think impaired circulation.

If one hand is warm and has a bluish tone, the circulation is worse on the side of the body where the hand is blue. Someone with this condition should be referred immediately to an internist or cardiologist, as this is the sort of problem which can get worse suddenly without warning.

If either or both hands are cold and blue, there is a local circulation problem. (Warm blue hands mean that the problem affects the entire body.) Cool bluish hands can be caused by frostbite or by nervousness. If only one part of a hand is cold, blood supply to that area is blocked; consult a physician.

If the hands are cold, clammy and bluish, the person may be in traumatic shock. If he's just been in an accident or had a tremendous emotional upset, put a blanket under him, make him lie down, give him a small glass of water, cover him loosely and call a doctor. If he stops breathing, give mouth-to-mouth resuscitation.

If the hands are pale, then suspect the person is anemic. Another test for anemia is to flex the fingers backward so the skin is stretched tightly across the palm. If the lines are pale or blue, he has an iron deficiency. Advise him to get a complete blood count to confirm the diagnosis and then see a nutritionist or holistic doctor about improving his diet. Although medical doctors are highly skilled in certain subjects, they are rarely trained in nutrition.

Another possible reason for pale lines in a flexed hand is internal bleeding. If the person has any reason to suspect he is bleeding inside, suggest he go to the doctor now and finish the palm reading later.

Pale hands can also be caused by excessive use of tobacco, by anxiety or unstable circulation. The skin of heavy smokers frequently has a gray, congested look.

Sometimes people with no specific illness have pale hands. Although they may not be clinically anemic, they are spiritually anemic. Cool, detached, dry, and unemotional—give these fellows the benefit of the doubt by suggesting that their problem is caused by some physical deficiency, and advise them to improve their diet, get more vigorous exercise, and "have a heart."

Redness limited to the parts of the palms which usually come in contact with surfaces can imply cirrhosis of the liver or, if the person is a woman, pregnancy. Or, they could have been sitting on their hands just before letting you look!

If the hands are red all over, a variety of interpretations is possible. Dishpan hands, hands of those who work with powerful chemicals, and hands chapped by prolonged exposure to cold weather are all red and rough. If they're red and tender, the person might be sunburned. Never overlook the obvious. On the other hand, if the backs of the hands are a vicious bright red, he could have pellagra, a rare vitamin deficiency disease.

Red hands on an apparently healthy body are associated with an excitable, overindulgent temperament; if the red hands are thick and fleshy, this person is prone to heartburn, indigestion and high blood pressure. His current state of pseudo-health will not continue unless he reduces the amount of meat, spicy foods and liquor in his diet.

Yellow palms can have either serious or boring causes. On the serious side we have jaundice or pernicious anemia. On the boring side we have callouses brought on by work, sports or eating too many carrots. (It is true that eating a lot of carrots can turn your skin yellow.)

Hand Weather: Temperature and Humidity

The proverb "cold hands, warm heart" could easily be rewritten, "cold hands, cold room" or "warm heart, cold feet." The temperature and dampness of the hands are frequently determined by the environment and by the person's level of relaxation. Ideally, the hands should be pink, and neither wet or dry; this shows good circulation, relaxation, and a healthy body equilibrium. Many people who are usually relaxed get nervous at the prospect of having their hands read. This is the Heisenberg Principle of Palmistry: The fact that you're reading the palms might cause them to change. If you hold the hands gently and project love toward the person as you bend each finger, you'll find that all hands involved get warmer. If you don't notice whether the hands are cool or warm, they are probably normal.

Hand temperature and dampness are closely related to the endocrine system, which excretes the hormes which regulate our moods, reproductive cycles and metabolism. Since the endocrine system also has a powerful influence on our behavior patterns, the texture and dampness of the skin give some clues to the temperament. Conversely, a person's temperament often reflects the functioning of his endocrine system. There is no precisely normal level of hormones in the body. Each person creates an equilibrium that works for him, and most people's systems work within about the same range of hormone levels. Some people's hands are always a little warm; others' are always a little bit cool. That doesn't mean they're sick—that's just the way their bodies work. Only if you see extremes of heat and cold should you send your friend packing to the doctor's office.

If the person's hands are always hot and sweaty, it indicates an overactive thyroid gland. The hands of someone who truly has a hyperthyroid condition are *never cold*. The nails are satiny and the palms are usually dripping with sweat. Never shake hands with a hyperthyroid person unless you have a tissue in your pocket. Hyperthyroid fingers are often long and bony, and the person is likely to be active, hardworking and excitable.

If the hands are hot and dry, it indicates a fever. Put your hand on the person's forehead. If it feels really hot, call his mother, spouse or doctor, as the situation demands.

If the hands are cold, doughy and dry, it indicates an underactive thyroid gland (hypothyroid condition). The fingers are usually sausage-shaped with sharply tapering tips. The nails are often brittle; they grow slowly. In moderate cases, the person will be self-indulgent, addicted to easy living and lacking in self-discipline. In extreme cases, hypothyroid people tend to be lethargic and overweight.

Many overweight people would like to attribute their fatness to a thyroid problem, but in fact the bulk of obesity cases is not caused by thyroid deficiencies: They are caused by eating too much and exercising too little. There's no need to criticize fat people about their weight, but don't encourage the belief that their problems are not their fault.

The great majority of people fall within the range of normal endocrine function. One moment of hot, sweaty hands does not brand someone a hyperthyroid. If you think you might have a severe case of thyroid imbalance, consult an endocrinologist. For less severe problems there are yoga postures which tone the whole endocrine system, including the thyroid gland. If there is a yoga teacher in your community, talk to him or her.

The Fishy Handshake Syndrome

In cases of acute shock, the hands are cold, clammy and bluish. "Shock" in the medical sense means a sudden loss of blood pressure following a severe trauma. However, some people are in a mild state of shock all the time. If the skin texture, finger shape and color are in the normal range but the hands are always cold, then the person is chronically nervous. Having cold extremities in stressful situations is a holdover from an evolutionary mechanism for dealing with danger. When an animal is cornered and fears a deadly attack, blood is instantly shuttled to the vital inner organs where it is most necessary for preserving the animal's life. Since a greater than usual supply of blood is huddled in the center of the body, the extremities get cold. Man, being a thinking animal, often has these visceral reactions to dangers which spring only from his own mind. Thus, someone who always has cold hands and a nervous air is in the same physical state as a fox cornered by hounds. Suggest that he breathe very deeply and slowly and imagine warmth and relaxation flowing into his hands. Tell him a funny joke. Then maybe he'll be better able to cope with the fears that froze in his hands.

Stiff and Painful Joints

Arthritis is the most common cause of painful joints in the fingers and hands. There are two major kinds of arthritis: osteoarthritis and rheumatoid arthritis. According to Dr. T.J. Berry, approximately 5 percent of all people over 40 have some symptoms of osteoarthritis; women outnumber men in a ratio of about ten to one. The symptoms are small painful knots at the top end of the middle joint. These often twist the fingers into the characteristically gnarled arthritic hand. A predisposition to arthritis is inherited, but proper diet and a healthy lifestyle can usually prevent it from developing and can improve dramatically even after it has set in. Some doctors will tell you arthritis is incurable and suggest surgery or strong drugs to help you cope with it. These extreme measures are often unnecessary. The only people we can definitely describe as incurably ill are dead people. If you have arthritis, or know someone who suffers from it, see a holistic health practitioner or a nutritionist. Read Paavo Airola's book, *There Is a Cure for Arthritis.* Imagine those knobs dissolving and leaving your hands young and limber again. There are alternatives to suffering, so why suffer?

Rheumatoid arthritis is less common than osteoarthritis, and can appear among younger people as well as the elderly. With proper treatment it can also be improved. In rheumatoid arthritis the lower finger joint stiffens up first; the upper joints are not affected until later.

"Funny" Fingers

Some abnormal finger shapes are congenital; others are acquired. Congenital variations include extra fingers, fingers joined together and abnormally bent fifth fingers. Some cases of clubbed fingers are inherited, but they are more likely to be caused by circulatory or glandular disorders. Extra fingers and toes are usually treated by surgical removal. A more serious condition is called *syndactyly*, which means that two fingers are stuck together in one skin. This can occur in people who are otherwise normal, but it also appears as part of a whole collection of other birth defects including congenital heart disease.

The fifth finger is sometimes called the little thumb, because so many revealing signs appear on it. The short little finger curved in toward the fourth finger is frequently seen among mongoloid idiots and is also associated with behavior problems. Studies by Friedmann and Wolff suggest that an extremely long, thin fifth finger signifies a predisposition to schizophrenia. Also, the "single digital flexion crease" is reported to be an infallible sign of mental weakness and flawed social adjustment. Normally there are several creases in the skin at the middle joint on the palmar side of each finger. The single flexion crease appears only on the fifth finger, where instead of the normal series of crinkles, there is only one stark line separating the bottom from the middle joint. A fairly normal person might have one of these signs, but if the abnormalities in the fifth finger are corroborated by deficiencies in the thumb and mounts then, cruel as it sounds, the person is a natural-born degenerate. That doesn't guarantee he's acting like one, but his natural inclination will always be to be stupid, maladjusted, and ill-tempered.

Clubbed Fingers

Not golf clubs, not nightclubs, not the Jack of Clubs. Just plain *clubs*—narrow at the bottom and wide at the top; those are clubbed fingers. Some people are born with them, but most who have them develop them because of impaired circulation or, more rarely, endocrine imbalance. Your first question when you see them should be, "Does this run in your family?" If it does, drop the discussion right there. If not, then look for the physical imbalance that made the fingers club.

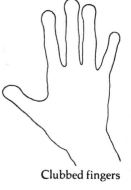

Clubbed fingers

Clubbed fingers are occasionally associated with pituitary obesity. This is a rare condition in which the pituitary, the master endocrine gland of the body, falls down on the job and causes disruptions throughout the body. Clubbed fingertips are not a principal diagnostic sign of this condition, but if someone suspects his pituitary is malfunctioning, he belongs in the hands of a competent endocrinologist, not a medical palmist. I have seen only one other case in which an endocrine imbalance caused clubbed fingertips. A struggling body builder took heavy doses of cortico-steroids as part of his athletic program. His biceps looked good for a few months, but his hands are permanently disfigured, with extremely clubbed fingertips on both hands; he altered the delicate hormone balance of his body, and his body showed him what it thought of his plan.

If clubbed fingers are neither inherited nor caused by endocrine imbalance, they are a sign of cardiovascular disturbance. If they appear suddenly in a normal hand, see an internist. According to Dr. Berry, there are two categories of clubbed fingers. In one, the fingers are dusky red and seem to be filled with blood; this is caused by excessive flow of blood to the fingertips, and appears most often in cases of congenital heart disease. In the second type, the clubbed fingers are paler. Chronic lung disease is more often responsible for this condition. The most easily recognized form of this type of clubbing is the Hippocratic finger, which has been associated since ancient times with chronic pulmonary tuberculosis. The index finger is usually the first to be affected—the middle joint becomes very thin and the top joint becomes clubbed and is covered with the "watch-glass" or Hippocratic nail. This nail is shiny and smooth and curves over the top of the finger at least halfway across the tip. Clubbed fingers return to normal after the lung or heart disease is cured.

Shaking Hands

Tremors occur for a variety of reasons, the most common of which are ordinary fear or anxiety. Before attributing any fancy meanings to your subject's trembling hands, be sure to consider the possibility that he's nervous. Suggest that he take a deep breath, and hold his hands briefly in your own (providing you're not nervous, too!) and picture him calming down. If the tremor continues throughout the reading, it might be one of these:

Familial A fine trembling that runs in families. It generally happens in middle-aged men under emotional stress and has no awful significance.

Parkinsonian A coarse, rapid, "pill-rolling" movement which occurs in victims of Parkinson's disease.

Cold If someone has just been out in cold weather or working in a walk-in freezer, his hands may tremble. This is because the body is trying to generate heat as rapidly as possible, and motion produces heat.

Intention An intention tremor is one which only appears when a person's hand approaches an object, for example, when he's picking something up or trying to touch his nose. This is an important sign of many diseases of the brain and nervous system.

Toxicity People whose bodies are poisoned by excessive intake of alcohol and drugs often have a chronic, fine tremor. This tremor continues even when they are not actively involved in poisoning themselves, and thus it is one way of telling whether someone is really on the wagon. Environmental or occupational toxins such as heavy metals can also cause this tremor. It disappears after the person has been fully detoxified. However, if the individual is merely between drinks or fixes, the tremor will continue.

Hyperthyroid This condition sometimes produces a fine trembling which gets worse when the person spreads his fingers wide apart. It is accompanied by the characteristic satiny skin and warm wet hand.

Hypoglycemia When hypoglycemic people go too long without eating, their blood sugar drops sharply and they feel anxious, depressed and irritable until they eat something to restabilize their blood sugar. Their hands might also tremble; this is most likely to develop several hours after the previous meal. Give the person a little fruit juice (no refined sugar!). If the tremor disappears, you know it was caused by hypoglycemia. If not, keep sleuthing.

Liver   Liver tremors are coarse and rapid, similar to those seen in Parkinson's disease. They get worse and begin to resemble a wing-beating motion if the person holds his arms out at his sides. Don't laugh. This is an early sign of liver damage which continues as long as the liver is in trouble.

These are the most frequently seen tremors. Just be sure that, before you pack someone off to Alcoholics Anonymous or a medical clinic, you're sure he isn't trembling from cold or from fear.

Diagnosis Through the Nails

Examining the nails is a fast and accurate method of gauging general health. Many systemic illnesses express themselves through changes in the nails; the onset of an illness or injury can even be dated within a four-month period by noting where on the nail the disturbance begins. See what you're missing if you wear nail polish all the time?

The nails are the first tissues of the body surface to develop; they sometimes appear as early as the ninth week of prenatal life. They are made basically of the same ingredients as the skin and have a lot in common with the hair; when general vitality is low, both the hair and the nails lose their luster. Although they might be nothing but vestigial claws from our days of tearing apart raw meat with our bare hands, the primary function of the nails now is the protection of our magnificent sense of touch.

The nails can develop several types of problems. They can grow abnormally, they cannot grow at all, or something can grow on them as in the case of fungus infections. All these problems can develop because of localized nail diseases, disruptions in the acid base balance of the body, or because of diseases which involve the entire system. Diseases of the nails are outside the focus of this book. Nevertheless, here's one little tip: Nail fungi might be cured by determining what kind of bug it is and whether it thrives best in an acid or an alkaline environment. Go on a short fast to change your body pH so that your body becomes inhospitable to the fungus. A medical laboratory and a nutritional doctor can help you with this. For treatment of nail disorders, see a dermatologist.

Healthy nails are pink, smooth and slightly lustrous. These are signs that the body has enough protein, the blood supply to the nail bed in adequate, and the person is free of undue stress. As in other aspects of medical palmistry, no one sign is a sure indicator of a specific illness; corroborating evidence is necessary before you venture a guess about the exact problem. When you do venture a guess, remember that that's what it is—an educated guess, not a medical diagnosis. As a medical palmist you can do a great service by referring people to the right source when you see they need help.

That means sending sick people to a doctor, malnourished people to a nutritionist, and so forth.

Color of the Nails (sans buff and polish)

Blue or Bluish Nails If all the nails are bluish the person has either just come in from a snowstorm or has a systemic circulatory problem. Blue skin always indicates an inadequate supply of oxygen in the blood.

If all the nails on one hand are bluish, the circulatory blockage is worse on the blue-handed side of the body. Have it checked soon by a doctor.

If only a few nails are bluish, the implications are less serious. They imply a localized disruption of circulation which might be temporary. They could also be relics of an old frostbite injury.

People with a cool disposition and no complaint of circulatory problems often have bluish nails. I like to think they act coolly because of a latent circulation problem, but it could be the other way around. If the nails are not bright blue but are just bluish, advise the person to get more vigorous exercise.

Red Nails All the factors that cause red skin cause red nails. These include hypertension, overexcitement, and eating too much meat and spicy food.

Pale Nails Pale nails have the same significance as pale skin. Poor nutrition and weakened general vitality are the most common cause of pale nails unless the person has just had a serious accident, in which case they are a sign of traumatic shock.

Other Signs on the Nails

Beau's Lines Named after Dr. Beau, who first described them in 1846, these are transverse ridges beginning at the nail and growing outward. They form a palpable dent in the surface of the nail. These lines indicate acute infection, nutritional deficiency, or accidental traumas. Since a nail grows out completely in four months, physicians during World War I are said to have determined the date of injuries by referring to these ridges.

Sometimes you can guess the nature of the trauma by noting where the Beau's lines appear. If they're on the thumbnail the problem affects every aspect of the person's life. If they appear on the Jupiter or Saturn fingers, then the problem related to or was caused by the person's work or other outer-directed activity. If they show up on the fourth or fifth fingers, the problem was deeper seated and related to the person's inner life and vital organs. If

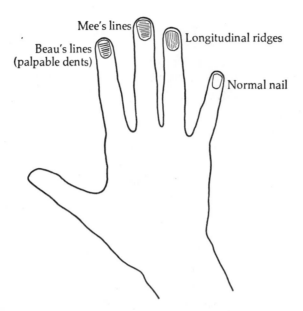

they appear on every finger, the person was completely traumatized by whatever happened to him at that time.

Mee's Lines   These are also transverse bands, but without the dent in the nail surface. They indicate high fever, arsenic and thallium poisoning, and some nutritional insufficiencies.

Longitudinal Ridges   These are associated with chronic stress and illness or with senility. In particular, they are seen in chronic colitis, rheumatism and hyperthyroidism, as well as with long-standing skin disorders. Longitudinal ridges are signs of chronic illness while Beau's and Mee's lines show brief periods of acute illness.

White Spots   These appear during periods of extreme fatigue or tension. They're also related to nutritional deficiencies, particularly calcium deficiencies, and to cirrhosis of the liver. If you suspect cirrhosis, look for yellow palmar surfaces as a substantiating sign. If they are brought on by a particularly difficult period of life, they disappear when the strain eases.

Hippocratic, or "Watchglass" Nails   These nails curve halfway around the fingertip and are shiny and round like watchglasses. When nails take on the watchglass shape the fingers often become so thin that the whole finger looks like a drumstick. Hippocratic nails are signs of chronic pulmonary tuberculosis and other chronic diseases of the circulatory and respiratory system. The nails return to normal after the disease is cured.

"Smoker's" Nails

A milder form of Hippocratic nails is seen among heavy smokers. This is not surprising, considering the crippling long-term effect smoking has on the lungs. If you see the nails beginning to curve around the fingertips you can be certain that the individual either has a hereditary weakness of the lungs, is a smoker or has recently quit smoking.

Spoon Nails   Spoon nails look hollowed out, like spoons. They appear in several endocrine disorders including hyperpituitarism and hypothyroidism as well as in iron deficiency anemia, chronic skin disorders and nutritional deficiencies.

Complete Loss of Nails   Some diseases such as scarlet fever, syphilis, leprosy, baldness, and exfoliative dermatitis cause the nails to fall off. This can also be caused by chemical poisoning.

Soft, Easily Split Nails   These are related to dietary deficiencies, particularly deficiencies in protein and calcium, to contact with strong alkalis, endocrine disturbances, syphilis, and to chronic arthritis.

Irregular Growth, Split Ends, Crinkly Edges   Particularly if they are accompanied by mottled or blotchy skin, these nail problems imply cardiovascular disturbances such as arteriosclerosis. The crinkly nail surface is also related to anemia.

Signs on the nails are health indicators that anyone can see or touch, as are the other signs covered in this chapter—color, temperature, sweatiness, finger shape and dermatoglyphics. Learning to read them will help you maintain your health by spotting illnesses before they become serious, and by knowing what your inherited weaknesses are so that you can take extra care of your most vulnerable points. There are methods of healing which also emphasize early diagnosis, but which depend more on sensing and balancing the energy flows which are the underlying causes of health and disease than on treatment with surgery or drugs. Doctors from both camps want everyone to feel better. What the energy-oriented healers claim is that surgery and drugs would rarely be necessary if natural vitality were permitted to run freely through the body and mind. Through energy channeling, messages, and projecting warmth, love and life into the bodies of their patients, they are soothing the mental and physical pain of lifetimes. In some cases traditional medicine like that described in this chapter is appropriate, and in other cases healing like that in the next chapter is the best route: The healing energy of the universe is available to you in many forms, so look around, breathe deeply, and do what works best for you.

6

Healing Hands

Holistic healers use a variety of methods including physical pressure on sensitive points and healing from a distance to permit that loving energy to go where it's needed and nourish the unwell person. The natural state of humanity is health. In this chapter we'll examine some of the ways in which the hands are used to channel energy and promote this natural condition of love and vitality.

All holistic healing techniques involve the hands. Either the problem is diagnosed through points on the hands and wrists as in hand reflexology and Oriental pulse diagnosis, or it is treated through the hands of the healer, as with acupuncture, acupressure, chiropractic, massage, reflexology or psychic healing, which is also known as "laying on of hands."

Modern medicine is based on the study of sickness; holistic healing is based on the study of health. The basic principle of holistic healing is that dynamic life energy can be consciously channeled. Although modern medicine has worked wonders in emergency care, in surgery and in understanding the physical mechanics of illness, all this progress in curing infectious diseases has been counterbalanced by an increase in stress- and diet-related illnesses. The medical establishment is clearly not responsible for junk food and jammed subways, but it is equally clear that fundamentally modern health care is not working: Millions of people who can't say they're *sick* don't feel *well*, and those who are sick are cut up, drugged out, or told their problems are imaginary. How can this go on in a universe brimming with vitality and love waiting to be tapped?

You can improve your own health by consciously channeling your energy through self-hypnosis, meditation, self-massage and thinking positively. If you want, you can weaken your health through thoughtless habits, tensing muscles and vital organs into awkward patterns, or by dwelling on negative thoughts and expectations. The physical mechanics of illness are complicated, but the energy dynamics are simple: *Constricted energy flow breeds disease.* Unfortunately, people tend to slip into negative thought patterns (fear, despair, anger, etc.) unless they train themselves otherwise. Negative thought, or more commonly, lack of thought, causes more illness and unhappiness than all the germs in the world. Negativity is a form of contraction, and positivity is a form of expansion. Your hands contain energy connections to your entire body and mind. At the end of this chapter you will learn a healing hand massage that will help you stimulate those connections in your hands and the hands of your friends. Although a hand massage will not change your life unless you also change your diet, thought patterns and lifestyle, it's an easy place to begin; after all, your hands are right there at the end of your arms. As for positive thinking, begin by not clinging to sad or hateful thoughts, and then pause and consider that no matter how much you might want to change your life, *you are alive,* and that is wonderful beyond words.

Other people can channel your energy for you and, if you're trained, you can channel for your friends. Acupuncturists relieve energy blocks and stimulate weak organs by inserting fine needles at focal points of energy on the body, and acupressurists do it by pressing hard on the same points. Reflexologists work by remote control, stimulating points on the hands, feet and ears to send energy to every part of the body. Chiropractors open blocked nerves by adjusting the spine with their hands. Homeopathic and naturopathic doctors treat with herbs or minute doses of other substances; nearly all of them augment these treatments with techniques such as acupuncture or chiropractic.

Psychic Healers

Although many psychic healers use their hands in their work, none would say that the hands actually heal. In fact, all the healers I know of say that the healer does not heal; in fact, no one "heals" anyone else. The healer acts as a channel opening the way for the individual to heal herself or, some people believe, for God or Divine Love or whatever name is chosen to do the healing. In psychic healing the hands are lightning rods conducting life energy through the healer into the body and spirit of the patient. You can see by the diversity of hands on the following pages that people of many different temperaments can be healers. Each works in his or her own way and according to his or her own beliefs. Despite this diversity of methods and ideas, several principles are constant, and the success rate of those who follow these principles is always high. The two main principles are:

1) Illness is caused by constricted energy flow at some level of the person's being, and

2) The healer herself does not heal.

Beyond these basics, there are two major camps in healing circles.

Some, such as Rosalynn Bruyere of the Healing Light Center in Glendale, California, study physiology and pharmacology in addition to reading auras and contacting spirit guides as preparation for healing. Thus, when she or one of her staff healers lay hands on a patient, they are consciously directing various frequencies of energy through their hands in accordance with a systematic knowledge of the physical and astral body of the patient. Nevertheless, Healing Light staff healer Rudi Noel says that every healing is a miracle to him. Like a child's birth, you know how it happened, but the knowledge doesn't diminish the magic.

Other healers work from a standpoint of religious faith. They hold their hands over the patient and let God do what He wants. Another excellent healer, Dr. Corrie van Loon of the Omni Foundation, says he does not diagnose or name illnesses, as he recognizes that it is everyone's right to be healthy, and he therefore "allows right action to take place." He does not instruct the energy where to go, but rather allows it to migrate to the areas where it's needed most. Dr. van Loon, Rev. Bruyere and her healers, and many others are credited with facilitating miraculous cures, so they must be doing something right. Mr. Noel says that both the systematic and the traditional schools have the same high success rate. As always, the watchword is *do what works*.

I wish I could show you the energy field of each of these healers through their prints. Each one has a unique force field around his or her hands, and each one shows the natural tendencies which they developed in order to become healers. Rosalynn Bruyere has the long pointed hands of a spiritual medium, and she does receive impressions from the "other side" when healing. Yet Rudi Noel, a staff healer at the center Bruyere founded, has more practical hands and has no spirit guide. He says he doesn't seek out spirits because "they have my number, they can call me." Noel and Bruyere are both successful healers. Dr. van Loon's square hands show that he could have been a businessman as well as a psychic, and in fact this is the case. He worked as an interior designer for many years before taking on spiritual work as a full-time vocation. (He was a professional psychic before becoming an interior designer, however.) Dr. An Thanh shows such sensitivity around the Girdle of Venus that I thought he must be overwhelmed by psychic impressions. His long practice of Buddhist meditation and his strong fate line helped him order this wealth of information.

Rev. Rosaline Bruyere, founder of the Healing Light Centers in Los Angeles, has participated in extensive laboratory research which verifies the fact that energy is transferred through healer to patient during healings. Demand for her assistance is so great that she now spends much of her time acting as a consultant for other healers.

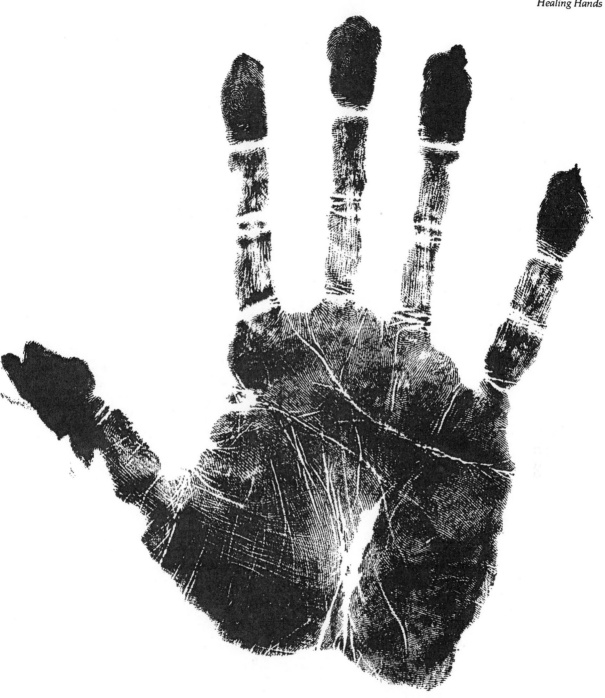

Rudy Noël, currently of the Healing Light Centers in the Los Angeles area, worked as an entertainer and as a reflexologist before devoting himself fully to his natural healing abilities. The power in his hand is intense, and he works from a standpoint of love for every patient.

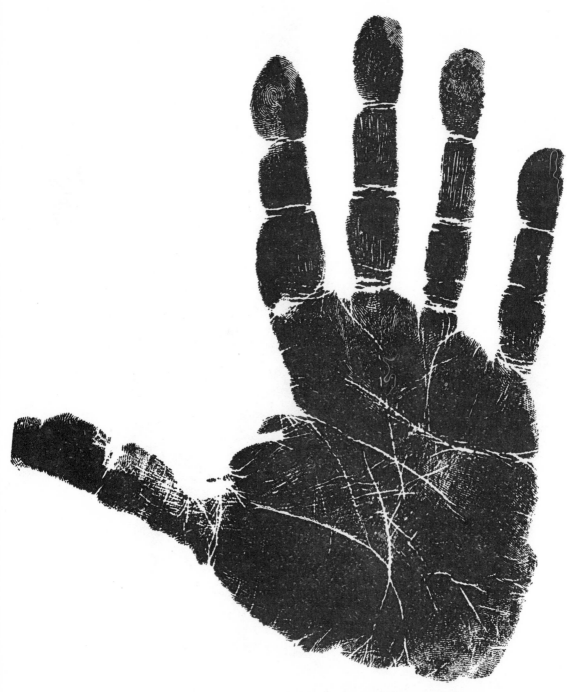

Dr. Corrie van Loon, founder of the
Omni Foundation in Santa Monica, California, worked as a professional psychic
and as a businessman for many years
until he merged his life with his fate by
taking up healing and teaching full-time.

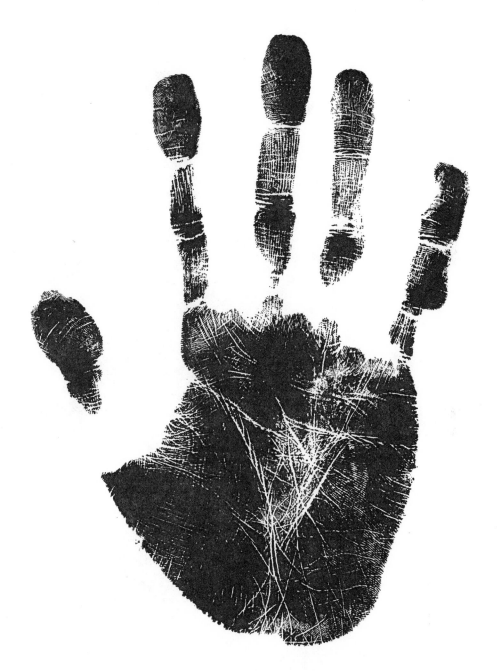

Thich An Thanh, M.D., uses the extreme
sensitivity and electrical energy of his
hands in his practice of nutritional and
herbal medicine in Los Angeles. In addition to being a licensed doctor of medicine,
he is a Buddhist monk.

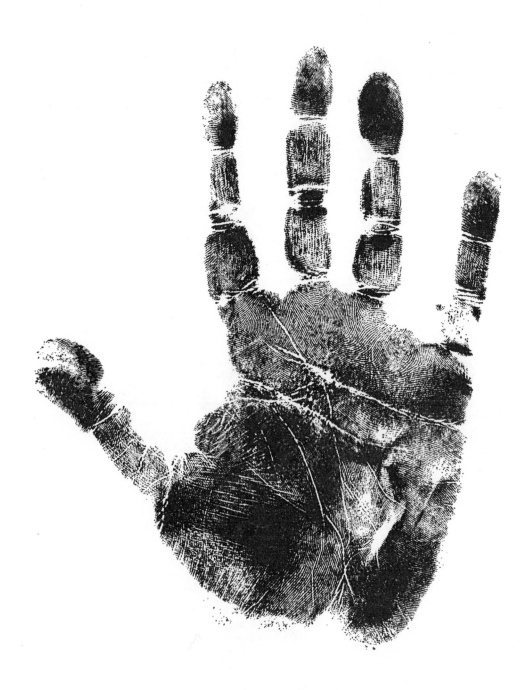

Roger C. Hirsh, B.Ac. (UK) C.A is an
acupuncturist, martial artist and researcher in Oriental medical sciences who fo-
cuses on traditional medical arts.

Jas Want Singh Khalsa, M.D., is an American Sikh physician practicing holistic medicine in Los Angeles. He uses behavioral kinesiology, Voll electro-acupuncture, herbs, and nutrition in his medical practice.

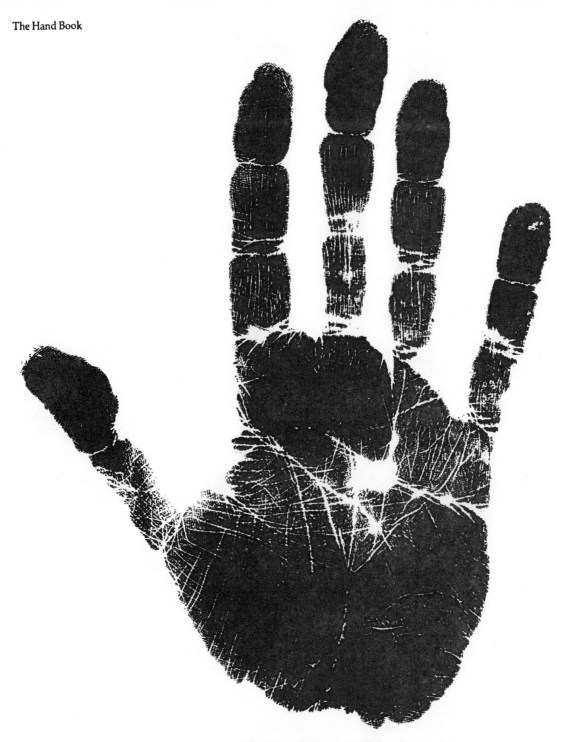

Dr. Giovanni Boni, MSDC, augments his psychic healings with chiropractic, homeopathy, acupuncture, and nutritional advice. Note the many lines of influence on the mount of Luna and the powerful inner life line.

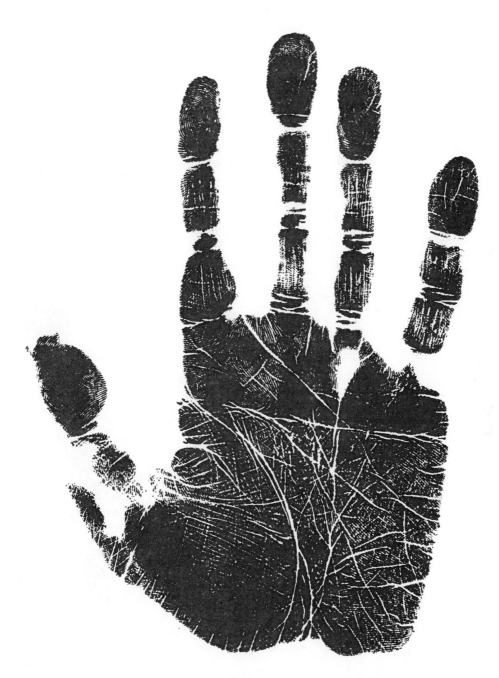

Jonathan Krown developed the ability to
heal after many years of practice in self-
awareness. He is able to transfer energy
to individuals in a way that dramatically
expands their consciousness as well as
improves their physical health.

Dixie Munroe has had the gift of healing since she was a child. Even people with no psychic training at all feel the energy when she enters a room. People wait months for a chance to see her.

Every healer shows some mark which could have led him or her to take up healing work. However, there is no one thing that all have in common, at least nothing that shows up in the print. What I see from having met and read the hands of all these people is that each of them is intensely dedicated to the work, each heals with a feeling of love for the patient, and each has a powerful energy field. This means healers are not a special race of chosen beings. They come from all backgrounds and work in a variety of ways. Although these men and women have devoted years, perhaps lifetimes, to the cultivation of healing skills, you, too, have the capacity to heal yourself.

Going through Channels

Acupuncture is the Oriental art and science of increasing circulation by inserting needles and/or burning moxa (mugwort) at specific points in the body, and by using herbs, nutrition, and psychological counseling. It is easier to harmonize the energy flows at acupuncture points because the electrical resistance of the skin drops dramatically near them. Most acupuncture points run in channels below the skin, called meridians. These meridians are like flexible pipes connecting distant parts of the body. If you release a blockup somewhere in the plumbing, the effects echo through the whole system. There are seventy-two meridians, of which fourteen are considered main meridians. Most of these major meridians can be monitored by taking the pulse on both wrists—six points on the right and six on the left. These major energy channels on the pulses are: small intestine, gall bladder, heart, liver, and kidneys on the left; and large intestine, stomach, triple warmer (regulator of body heat), lungs, spleen, and circulation/sex on the right. By interpreting these twelve pulses, a skilled doctor can definitely sense how well all the organs in your body are working. Think how much it would cost you to have all these organs tested by a medical laboratory, and in the end you'd get the same basic information about what parts of your body are trouble zones. It takes many years to master pulse diagnosis, but the fact that the entire organism can be monitored so closely through the pulses is one more sign of how much can be learned from the areas around the hands.

Another way in which the hands provide sites of diagnosis and treatment for acupuncturists is through the meridians and special points which run through the hands. Six of the major meridians run through the fingers, and six run through the toes. The lung meridian travels down the thumb; the large intestine meridian runs down the index finger; the circulation/sex meridian courses through the third finger; and the triple warmer heats the fourth finger; the little finger has meridians coming and going; the heart meridian runs up the palmar side and the small intestine meridian runs down the back of the finger. Balancing these meridians at the hands is more powerful than treating them elsewhere in the body: Points in the lower arms and legs (particularly at the hands and feet) are known as command points, because the energy changes from a positive to a negative charge or vice versa when it reaches the ends of the meridians in the fingers and toes. It's like a pendulum which swings out to its limit on one side before swinging back to the other. If you want to change the frequency of the arc, catch it just as it's changing direction—that's where the swing is strongest and that's where you have the most control over its new frequency.

Despite the strength of the points on the hands and feet, acupuncture treatment is not complete unless points on the entire body are taken into consideration. A thorough discussion of acupuncture is beyond the scope of this book. If you are interested in learning about it, begin with the books of Lawson-Wood and Felix Mann. However, you can practice basic *acupressure* with a little training and a strong thumb. (Proficiency at acupressure massage also requires serious training, but it's safer to dig your fingers into someone's palms with minimal training than it is to sink needles.) In acupressure massage, firm pressure is put on the acupuncture points to stimulate energy flow.

A few acupressure points will be covered in the massage section of this chapter. Many books and workshops are available on the subject if you wish to explore it further. Jacques de Langre's books on Do-In and Iona Teeguarden's books on acupressure are excellent introductions. Acupressure is related to Japanese *shiatsu* massage.

Reflexology

When the doctor taps your knee with his little rubber hammer, you can't help but kick out because that tap sends an impulse straight to your spine and your spine sends a message straight back saying, "Punt!" You couldn't prevent it if you tried. Reflexology is based on the same principle, i.e., certain parts of the body are connected so that stimulating one part will automatically stimulate its related part. For example, according to reflexology theory, pressing a certain spot on your foot will automatically and instantly stimulate your pancreas, and pressing another spot will have the same effect as massaging your spine. The greatest concentrations of reflex points are found in the feet, hands and ears, although the irises of the eyes also reflect the condition of each area of the body. Although the foot is an extremely powerful site for reflex treatments, reflexology through the ears and hands is also beneficial. In cases of chronic illness or when the injury can't be touched because of infection or broken bones, reflexology treatments give dramatic results.

Theories differ on how reflex points are connected to the rest of the body, and it doesn't really matter. When reflexology works, it helps, and even if now and then it doesn't work, it doesn't harm. In healing and intuitive arts it's results that matter, not theories. However, here are a couple of explanations for your amusement. Mildred Carter, author of several texts on foot and hand reflexology, maintains that the reflex points are connected to the limbs and organs through a fine web of interlacing energy threads in the etheric field surrounding the body. Well, anything's possible!

A more systematic theory is presented by polarity balancer Richard Gordon. Polarity balancing theory is similar to acupuncture in that it assumes the body contains positive and negative electrical forces which must be balanced to maintain health, but it differs in that it works through balancing oppositely-charged energy fields rather than by tapping energy channels. That is, they'll balance an excess of positive energy by introducing negative energy and vice versa. All top sections in the body are positively charged, middle sections are neutral, and bottom sections are negative. The right side is positive, and the left side is negative.

Imbalances in any positively charged area are reflected in other positively charged areas; the same holds true for negative and neutral zones. Looking at the chart, you can see how this relates to the hands. The upper head is reflected in the fingertips, the nose and cheeks in the middle joint, and the mouth and jaw in the lower joint. This pattern of relationship continues down the hand with analogous connections to the rest of the body. From this theory you could deduce that soreness around the head line of the right hand indicates a disruption in one of the organs in the right side of the chest, and tenderness of the lower part of either hand indicates a problem in the digestive or reproductive systems. I've seen many cases where lower digestive upsets were relieved by massage to the lower part of the palm, although my experience indicates that soreness in the fingers is more likely to indicate blockage in acupuncture meridians than it is to problems in the head. As always, accept only the parts of these theories which your experience tells you are valid.

Still another form of palm reflexology comes from palmistry. If someone holds the hand out with one finger crowding another, it shows that the traits of the pushy finger are repressing the energy of the victimized one. This has been verified for me in countless palm readings. If the fingers naturally bunch up when the talents they represent are suppressed, it makes sense to train each finger to be supple and independent so that the talents associated with the finger will be strengthened. Imagine life energy as white—white contains all colors in the spectrum. Now imagine sexual energy as purple. If you put a purple filter over a white light, you get purple light. This lightbulb technology relates to the hands in this way: Sexual energy is stored in the mount of Venus, so the mount of Venus is like a purple filter. When you bring more life energy into the palm by conscious channeling and massage, the white light sailing through the mount of Venus turns purple and voila! More gusto.

This principle applies to every mount in the palm. Channeling energy to the mount of Apollo encourages artistic talent and success; channeling to Jupiter increases confidence and opportunities for financial success; infusions to Mercury stimulate verbal expression, and so on. When you see someone with a particularly desiccated mount, encourage her to give extra love and attention during her hand massage, and to picture energy flowing into that mount till she can't see over the top of it. In my experience this sort of massage combined with straightening and strengthening all the fingers has a distinctly positive effect on the person's life. Whether this effect is actually due to a redistribution of Apollonian or Venusian energy or is due to the person's thinking about improving herself every time she massages her hands is irrelevant. What matters is that she feels better in the end.

In places, hand reflexology, polarity zone therapy, and palmistry contradict each other or are completely unrelated. You might wonder how these different explanations can all be true, since they all refer to the same hands. It's because there are no rigid truths when you are dealing with individuals and with the inner sense.

Different explanations are true at different
times for different individuals.

A tension pattern which means blocked sinuses one day might indicate blocked artistic talent another. That's why I suggest that if you want to be a really accurate palmist, you study everything in this book so closely that you can nearly recite it, and then forget it completely when you actually read someone's hands. Not everything can be figured out, but everything can be known. Let logical contradictions stay in your mind if you must, but keep love in your heart and deep breath in your abdomen, and your readings will always be appropriate to the person's needs at the instant you read her.

Healing Hand Massage

Whether you'll be massaging your own hands or working on a friend's, always begin by taking several deep breaths. Turn your attention to your energy centers. Relax. Imagine all the warmth of the universe spreading through your body and into your hands. If you're working on a friend, see if you can sense the kinship between you, realizing that the unity you share is infinitely greater than any personal differences. Prepare to enjoy the massage. We'll begin with a basic warm-up massage which is complete in itself. After that you can do more specifically healing-oriented work by referring to the hand reflexology chart and the polarity zone chart and to a few acupressure points. Massage of the hands alone will not substitute for medical treatment or for necessary changes in diet and lifestyle. What it will do is send mild stimulation to every part of your body, toning your system and relaxing your mind. It is essential that you give each hand equal time. It's better to give half a massage to both hands than to massage all of just one. The most important thing, though, is to relax, breathe deeply, and enjoy.

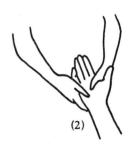

The Warm-Up

1) Put a very little bit of oil onto one of your hands and rub your palms together. Nearly any kind of oil will do, although Weleda brand oil or sesame oil are particularly good. If you can't find any oil, do without it (and hope your hands are sweaty). Take a few deep breaths. Feel that energy purring through your system.

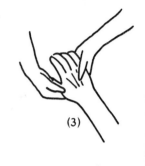

2) Take the person's hands into your hands or, if you're massaging your own hands, take your hand in your hand. Work the thumbs all over the palm, pressing them in and then moving them in little circles all over the hands.

3) Turn over the hand and work with the thumb or fingers up and then down the back of the hand. Work in the valleys between the tendons. These channels contain acupressure points and they open up the pathway from the wrist to the hand. Stop and press hard at regular intervals in the valleys, then glide your thumb smoothly up them from the wrist toward the fingers.

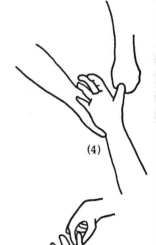

4) Then work the "webs" between all the fingers. Lots of tension huddles in these spots. Press each web between your thumb and index finger and rub back and forth. If they're sore, that is OK; try to keep rubbing till the soreness goes. It might not be possible to rub out all the tension in these sections in one massage, so if you can't rub it all out, move on.

Often you'll feel sharp edges as you press the webs, as though there were little crystals under the skin. These are caused by accumulated toxins which gather near all the joints. Kiss your poisons goodbye by massaging the crystals until they dissolve into the bloodstream and have a second chance at being excreted.

5) The fingers are next. First take hold of the thumb, holding it loosely by its tip. Twist it back and forth a little, then tug on it for a second and let it go. Apply this corkscrew and tugging motion to all of the fingers.

6) Press each fingertip hard between the thumb and index finger.

7) Now press hard on the sides of each phalange midway between the joints. Press in hard with your thumb and index finger, hold for 30-60 seconds or until you feel a release of tension.

8) Now for the finger stretch. If you're doing your own hands, lace the fingers of both hands together and then push your hands out away from your body so that those fingers are stretched nearly vertical. If you're doing someone else's hands, lace the fingers of one of your hands through her

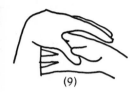

(9)

(10)

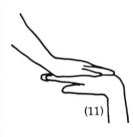

(11)

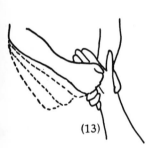

(13)

(14)

hands and stretch fingers back so they stand up as straight as possible without hurting her unbearably. Let them go slowly—no need to snap them. Be sure to keep the treatment equal on both hands.

9) Bend the thumb down so that it is nearly parallel to the wrist (the hand will bend down with it). According to Kundalini Yoga doctrine, any healthy flexible person will be able to bring her thumb to rest along her forearm. For most people this is quite painful, so don't force it—just give it the idea.

10) Take hold of the hand and squeeze the thumb side and the pinky side downward so that the whole hand ends up looking as wide as the wrist. Reverse the move and extend the hand backward pulling gently on both sides so that the hand looks like a flying bird.

11) Gently push the entire hand up until it forms nearly a right angle to the wrist. If this hurts, don't push much beyond the comfort zone. Reverse the maneuver, pressing the entire hand downward so that it forms a right angle in the other direction. The individual should be able to hold her hand parallel to the ground whether the arm is extended downward or pointed upward.

12) Take off your watch, if you didn't in the beginning. Did you ever play the "Hokey Pokey" when you were a child? Hokey Pokey is a sophisticated phrase for "wiggle your hands." Now, calling on your childhood experience, shake out your hands. Just let them go, shaking them up and down and right and left, until they feel as limp as children ready for a nap. You might find your arms waving as you waggle your hands; this is OK.

13) Remember pounding your little brother when you were a child? Call on that childhood experience and pound on your friend's palm. Use either your fingertips as a group, or a loose fist like that you'd use when knocking on a door. Pound the palm and lower fingers lightly for a few minutes; this will bring the blood to the surface.

14) For the final flourish, hold each hand between both of your hands. Take a few deep breaths and become aware of every part of the hand that is touching yours. Feel the energy flowing between your hands and the hand of your friend. Hold this position for a little while, or until you feel the energy ebb, and then repeat it with the other hand. Place both of your hands softly on your friend's hands and slowly remove them.

15) Sit quietly for a moment.

Feel free to improvise movement as the moment requires, or to stop and let the energy rearrange itself before beginning another move. When two hands meet, they set up their own relationship apart from the intellectual relationship between two minds. Let them follow their own course. If your attention is centered with affection and your breath is deep and full, your hands will know where to go. Nevertheless, the movements suggested above are worth practicing until they become second nature. The heart can bring forth passionate speech, but before we can speak we must learn words. These basic moves are a simple vocabulary. Let your heart guide you to create a poetic massage.

PALM REFLEXOLOGY

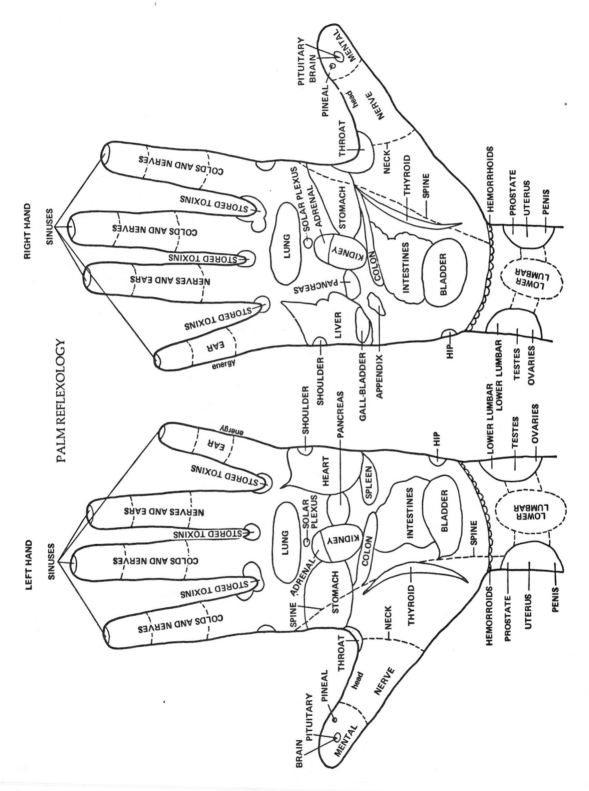

Rub Your Blues Away

All massage is therapeutic in a sense, but in reflexology and acupressure there is an explicit intention to heal. To perform a hand reflexology treatment, familiarize yourself with the reflexology chart and work over every point of it. Press down hard with your thumb and follow Mildred Carter's maxim, "If it hurts, rub it out." This is not a Mafia slogan, but rather expresses the belief that pain signals blocked energy and blocked energy means disease. The only exception to the rub-it-out rule is in the center of the palm which corresponds to the glandular system. These areas are extremely sensitive so don't overmassage them at first. On other areas, however, rub that pain right out of your hands.

You probably hit many acupressure points during the warm-up and reflexology massages, but there are a few special acupressure points on the hands worth mentioning. It would be misleading to imply that acupressure treatment takes place only on the palm—it is a form of deep body massage which incorporates points on the entire body. However, acupressure points on the hands are linked through meridians with all other parts of the body, so it is possible to do a general stimulation or calming treatment through the hand. According to Jacques de Langre, a leading authority on Do-In acupressure, soft, stroking movements stimulate and deep, slow pressure sedates. The most powerful effects always come from deep pressure. If you're interested in learning more about acupressure massage for the entire body, begin with Mr. de Langre's books, or those of Iona Teeguarden.

Whenever you do a deep massage to the fingers, you are stimulating the major meridians and acupressure points. In addition to the major meridian points, a few spots on the palm are particularly useful:

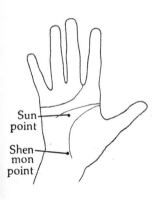

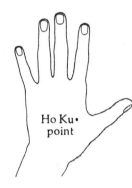

Ho Ku point

Sun point

Shen mon point

On the axial tri-radius (Shen-man point) — Pressing deeply on this point calms the nerves and relieves insomnia and hysteria.

At the very center of the palm — The so-called "sun point." Pressing here energizes the whole body.

On the back of the hand, deep between the thumb and index finger (Ho-ku point) — Good for what ails you. Headaches, colds, and sore throats are eased after this point is used. Remember it when the weather gets bad.

At some times sore spots would be associated with the acupuncture meridians running through them and at other times the reflexology chart is the one to use. Follow the prescriptions of your inner voice when choosing a treatment, and you won't go wrong. If your inner voice is not clear, then work on deep breathing and wait for it to become clear before you try to fix anybody else. Again, let me reiterate that hand massage is not a substitute for competent medical care, but it is a tool for toning your body and calming your mind.

I hope that this chapter has increased your awareness of your own healing abilities, shown you how your hands serve as tools of diagnosis and of treatment, and made it clear that you have the ability to heal yourself in many ways; healers use their hands only as channels, and even then they don't *make* anyone better—they're just skilled at letting the healing happen.

Your hands are instruments of magic. Keep them soft, flexible, and relaxed and life will sing through them to the rest of your body/mind. When you look at your hands and work on them, think of everything they contain and everything they represent—connections to all your vital organs, evidence of how fully you are using your innate talents, and signs of how gracefully you move. Your face, your feet, your eyes and your posture all tell the secrets of personality and health which you think no one else knows, but your hands are always in *front* of your eyes, not beside them or beneath them, so they are tools for self-knowledge. Look at them and learn, remember what they're telling you about possibilities for expansion and health. Let your hands remind you what a miracle it is to be human and to be alive. Health and happiness are ever-present; only our concerted efforts at staying miserable keep us down.

A Zen text, by the Zen master Hakuin, *The Song of Zazen,* sums up the needlessness of clinging to all forms of disease:

> All beings are primarily Buddhas.
> Like water and ice,
> There is no ice apart from water;
> There are no Buddhas apart from beings.
> Not knowing how close the Truth is to them,
> Beings seek for it afar—what a pity!
> It is like those who being in water
> Cry out for water, feeling thirst.
> It is like the rich man's son,
> Who has lost his way among the poor.
>
> . . .
>
> At this moment what is there that you lack!
> Nirvana presents itself before you,
> Where you stand is the Land of Purity.
> Your person, the body of Buddha.

When you look at your hands, remember your humanity. When you touch another with your hands, feel your heart. And if the smallest healing takes place through your hands, give thanks.

7

Palm Listening

When you're listening, your mind is poised and alert; your attention is focused, yet your mind is open. The ears always hear, but the eyes only see where you look. In palmistry, listening is more important than looking. In the previous chapters you've learned what to look for in the hands, but it is the open listening to the message of the palm that makes the difference whether you become a rigid, by-the-book reader or an accurate, intuitive interpreter of the hands. It's actually easier to listen than to look, because when you look you must know what to look *for*, but when you listen all you have to do is keep your mind receptive. Master the basics and then forget them. They'll sink into the water table of your unconscious mind and return to the surface as natural springs of intuition when you contact the hands you want to read. Then the palm will be reflected through your educated intuition.

As you practice more, your intuition will blend with your textbook knowledge into accurate palm listening. In the meantime, here are a few general principles that I have found helpful in reading or listening to palms.

The whole arrangement of a palm reading, where one person lets another person study a part of his body and then make pronouncements about his personality and future, lends itself to several misconceptions. First, the palm reader might feel powerful, which would be a mistake since he's not telling the subject anything the subject doesn't already know, and the person being read might fall under the deluded impression that the palm reader has some special powers. We know that this is false too, since everyone is innately intuitive and anyone can learn to read palms. However, what someone thinks is true is just as powerful as what actually is true, so remember to negate these two fallacies every time you run across them in yourself or in others. It also helps if you explain to the subject the general principles of palmistry, including how you come to your conclusions.

Even people who claim they don't believe in palm reading remember their readings for years, so be careful what you say. The person whose hands you're reading is listening closely to you. He's trusting you, and the more he trusts you the more responsibility to him you have. The more accurate your readings become, the more responsibility you have not to "blow people's minds" indiscriminately.

The most essential principle in palm reading is this: *Cause no pain.* Everyone who comes to you comes with his hands open; he is opening himself to you simply by letting you read his hands. After you refine your intuition and master the principles in this book, you will be able to discern some of those emotional "magic buttons" that can make a person explode. Everyone has their personal tragedies—the exciting trips they never got around to; the nervous breakdowns and disappointments in love and in business; the deaths of loved ones; and the pervasive loneliness they just can't shake. Why rub it in? Sometimes you will see the mere simplicity and averageness of someone's life; this can be a source of pain to someone who has, for example, a strong Jupiter finger which says he would have loved to do more. If you are going to open old wounds by bringing them up in detail, have a growth-oriented reason for what you say, and say it compassionately. Even if you think what you have to say will be helpful or lead the person to greater self-insight, remember that good advice at the wrong moment is bad advice. If you have any doubts at all, keep your mouth shut; you don't have to tell everything you know. The more accurate your palm reading becomes, the more serious become your responsibilities for speaking clearly and compassionately.

Choosing Your Words

Before you know what words to choose, you have to know what you're going to say. That's not what you *want* to say, because if you begin by knowing what you want to say you're as fixated on yourself as the person who knows what he wants to hear. As a palmist your goal is to open yourself to the message of the palm and report it accurately and sensitively. Once you've mastered the basic principle that the palm reflects the energy of the person, and remembered the significance of the life line, head line, heart line, fate line, secondary lines, and are familiar with the meaning of all the mounts, you can let the palm speak to your intuition and then let your intuition speak through your mouth.

*The palm reflects the person and the
palmist reflects the palm.*

Your words, your tone of voice and your gestures are what the person will remember. To insure as much as possible that you communicate without causing misunderstanding or anxiety, remember to:

• Assess the person's age, probable educational background and emotional state and adjust your tone and vocabulary accordingly. Your reading will help you here. People with sharply curving head lines will find blunt statements hard to swallow and will probably exaggerate the gravity of what you say. Understate. Those with firm square hands and straightforward lines will be impatient if you don't get right to the point.

If you have any bad news, like a probable illness or an approaching island or bar in a major line, preface it with a statement about the person's capacity to change his own hands and life and with something good about the hands, such as a good basic shape or a strong thumb. You can find something positive to say about everyone. Many people overlook the fact that good and bad usually come together, and that good often comes ultimately from experiences which seem painful or unnecessary at the time they occur.

• In addition to your words, consider your tone of voice; it reflects the quality of your breathing. If your breath is deep and slow, then your voice is rich and low. It will have a comforting ring to the person you're reading for. Be aware of changes in your voice; if you start to speak rapidly you make it hard for the person to understand you. If your voice takes on a higher pitch, you're getting nervous. Slow down. You'll never get a clear beam on your intuition if words are tumbling from your mind and mouth in high-pitched shallow gasps. Initially, your tone of voice will have more emotional impact on the person than the meaning of the words you say, so don't squeak.

• You also influence your friend by your touch. Ideally, your hands will be warm, flexible and calming to him because you'll be confident enough of the intuition speaking through you that your ego will not be activated. However, realistically speaking, there are times when we all forget this and get cold, clammy and nervous. If you can't steady your breath and warm your hands, try to avoid doing the reading. If you can't avoid the reading, at least keep your hands off your friend.

• Ask for feedback. If you have the slightest suspicion that the person doesn't understand what you mean, ask him to repeat your statement back to you in his own words. Frequently he's gotten it all wrong. Keep talking back and forth until you reach an agreement between what you meant and what he understood. When you reflect someone's palms for them, what matters is *their understanding* of what you say, and the positive use to which your statements can be put in their everyday life.

While you're mastering the basics of palm reading, you might make some mistakes, so don't hesitate to ask for confirmation of your readings. By asking for feedback and remembering what led you to make your incorrect statements, you'll hone your abilities and develop your own feel for reading hands. If you know that you're a beginner, let the person who trusted you to read his hands in on the secret too.

• Never predict the date of death. One's death is one's own business. Even if you think you know when someone will die, say nothing. You might be wrong and the hands might change, but most of all, no one on earth has the right to create fear, or possibly a self-fulfilling prophecy, by guessing aloud about the time of someone else's death. It is irresponsible and absolutely inexcusable. Just assure the curious that they will eventually die and suggest they make the most of the time they have left, regardless of how long it is.

• Admit the possibility of error. Everybody makes mistakes. Perhaps you weren't paying attention, or spoke without considering your words, or simply misinterpreted something that you looked at carefully. You'll learn more, faster, if you admit the possibility of error. If someone tells you they really think you're wrong about a claim you've made, just say, "Perhaps I was mistaken . . ." and move on. If you were mistaken, you'll only get yourself in deeper by trying to justify yourself.

Another possibility when people tell you you're wrong is that you've tactlessly said something so true that the person is unable to accept it. In cases like these, let the person off the hook immediately by saying that it might have been you, the reader, who was mistaken. Ideally you'll be keenly enough attuned to the person for whom you're reading that you'll automatically delete or rephrase the items which trigger his defense mechanisms. By backing off after you hit a "magic button" you are showing that you respect him enough to accept his statements about himself and that you trust the universe enough that someone else will come along and say the same thing to him when he's able to act on it.

• Respect everyone equally. No matter how simple, boring or rude a person may seem to you, he is the only him he's got. The part of God that breathes through him is the same spark that breathes through you, so by respecting him you respect yourself. Let the God-spark in you meet the God-spark in your friend and your readings will always be full of affection and warmth.

• Remember that hands change. Why should they not change when everything else changes? Be sure the person you're reading for knows this as clearly as you do.

• Remember that everyone is responsible for his own life. Every individual can change his lines and mounts to some degree, and can maximize his use of his innate talents. That implies that you, the palmist, are not responsible for making anyone's decisions except your own, and you ought to be leery of advising people about specific decisions.

• Look for main themes. It would take hours to read every single detail of a palm and, unless he were supremely egomaniacal, your friend would become bored and impatient if you did. By looking for the main themes of a person's life, you can go straight to the central conflict or problem of his life without spending hours on details the person is not interested in.

Particularly if someone seeks you out or is quite willing to let you look at his palms, odds are that there's something he wants to hear from you or he has some problem on his mind. There's nothing startling about this—most people have a lot of things on their minds. The point is to address yourself to the main issue without touching on it so directly that you break rule number one about causing no pain.

Main themes are more than dilemmas like, "Should I move to a different city?" or "Should I go through with my divorce?" They are the central conflicts from which most other conflicts arise. They can be seen in the entire hand and they more or less permeate the person's life. Look at them as "karmic homework," or the conflicts we were put on earth to work out. They show themselves as imbalances in the hands. If you see that any quadrant is over- or underdeveloped, or any finger disproportionately long or short, you know the root of many conflicts. At other times the theme is less obvious. It can show up as a mismatch between the character of the lines and the shape of the hand (for example, frazzled lines on a powerful hand show strength to accomplish much, but incapacity to channel energy constructively) or as a contradiction between the shape of the hand and the form of the fingertips. Still another possibility is that one line, or even one place on a line, has created enough problems to color the entire life. A steeply curved head line, a chained heart line, or a tormented period in early life can create a lifetime's worth of anguish to be resolved.

Some people work consciously on their psychological and spiritual development. Through repeated confrontation with the central dilemmas of their lives, they break the grip of their major problems. The advantage of finding and confronting main themes is that once the problem is understood it can be resolved, and then the person feels a thousand times better than before he began. This positive aspect of negative experiences is something that many people overlook.

In rare instances you will not be able to find a main theme. Some people are born balanced and so their main theme is wondering why everyone else seems so mixed up. Others lead such simple and regulated lives they never

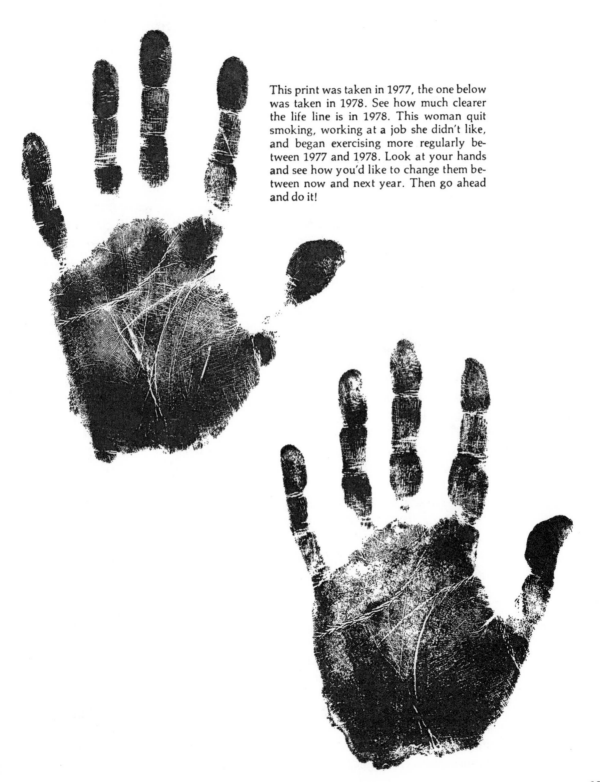

This print was taken in 1977, the one below was taken in 1978. See how much clearer the life line is in 1978. This woman quit smoking, working at a job she didn't like, and began exercising more regularly between 1977 and 1978. Look at your hands and see how you'd like to change them between now and next year. Then go ahead and do it!

sense inner conflicts. However, regardless of social or educational background, most people are both complicated and confused; if you can put your finger on the main problem they can get to work on it instead of wasting time on secondary conflicts. This is exactly like holistic medicine; it's useless to treat symptoms if the underlying problems are not treated at the same time. Go to the root.

Special Cases

As word gets around that you're studying palmistry, a wider variety of people may ask you for readings. "Wider variety" sometimes includes boring, pushy, egotistical, neurotic or hysterical people, as well as those with whom you feel zero natural rapport. These people are our brothers and sisters in the universe, and they deserve love and attention, too. However, the kind of attention they deserve is not always the kind they want. Here are a few pointers to help you deal with these special cases.

Some palms will set your inner voice off like a telegraph and others are going to leave you cold. You don't like everyone you meet, and you won't feel instant psychic rapport with every palm you read. Unfortunately, the palms that don't speak to you often belong to nice, eager people, best friends' grandmothers, and others who feel unsettled when a palmist glances at their palms and says, "Forget it." If you're confronted by a psychic dead fish, try not to show your reaction right away. If you can, excuse yourself from doing the reading. This is another case when "I'm not in the mood" provides an acceptable if unpopular response. However, if you really can't get out of it, take several deep breaths.

Remember that your intuition has not deserted you entirely; it just wants the day off. Try and convince it to take tomorrow instead. Breathe slowly, focus your attention on your center and remember that it might be really important to this person to have his palms read at this moment. This is called "priming the pump." Begin with a completely literal reading, just remembering what you've read in this book. That alone will be enough to satisfy most people, even if you know that you could be more precise if your intuitive voices were fully engaged. (You might find your intuitive juices start flowing halfway through the reading.)

There are only a few cases for which I have found it almost impossible to do any reading at all: for pushy people, for extremely dull people who've shut off their own natural vitality, and for people who think they can't change. Pushy people are the ones who come up to you in the middle of dinner or an interesting conversation and thrust their hands in your face commanding, "Read my palms!" Try to be polite even though the person doesn't deserve it. Who knows, he could be painfully shy and consider this the friendly outgoing approach. A good line for dealing with pushy people is this:

> "A really accurate palm reading requires at least half an hour of quiet, careful study. I would not be doing justice to you if I tried to do an off-the-cuff reading while I'm in the middle of doing something else." (This also has the advantage of being entirely true.)

You'll know the extremely boring people when you see them. They mean well, but what good does it do them? These people not only look boring and act boring, they usually have boring palms—a few weak lines, a paltry thumb and minimal vitality. Even though you respect their individuality and recognize them as your brothers in the community of living beings, etc., etc., there's nothing to *say* about them because they're so boring! At some level the boring person knows how nondescript he is, but he doesn't want to hear it from you. The advantage of boring people over rude people is that bores are usually satisfied with a few simple noncommittal statements like, "You must be very healthy in general," or, "I see you are very devoted to your husband/wife." Simple lives require simple descriptions, so as long as you keep it brief, these people won't cause you too much trouble.

However, boring people who think they are not boring begin to edge over into rude, so if you value your time and peace of mind, learn to keep these readings very short. Try "It's hard for me to say more without a very careful study." (This only works when you're standing in a train station) or, "Well, of course, anyone can become President these days . . . your palm doesn't indicate any future like that at the moment, but nothing's to stop you from entering the primaries." If the person is really bent on hearing you talk about his ego for hours, suggest he pay you highly for your time. An instant disappearing act usually follows. A subtle variation on the pushy routine comes from people who invite you out to dinner in order to hold their palms between the fork and your mouth. Try to spot this gambit before you accept the invitation. If you decide the dinner is worth it, consider the palm readings you do over coffee as payment for your supper. Do not pick up the tab.

A final hint about dealing with rude and boring people: Remember that you are the palm reader. If you stop talking with an air of finality, most people will lack the nerve to keep asking questions. Be patient for a few questions, but if someone is insecure enough to hound you with questions like, "Am I happy?" or "Will I make a million dollars?" your playing along will do more harm than good. End the reading firmly before you start to feel annoyed. Once you get annoyed, you'll have to spend the time and energy to relax yourself into an open state again. Is that person's ego gratification worth the trouble? More important, if someone is really pushy about such questions, he probably has some idea in mind that he wants you to support; he is not listening to you anyway.

A similar principle applies to people who complain about their current situation but are unwilling to change it. Some of these people love to suffer, and the rest are still building up the nerve to make a move. They may ask you for suggestions and then tell you everything you said is impossible. They can't change their diet or their lifestyle or get out of destructive relationships. Once you spot this trend, politely end the reading. It's pointless to make suggestions to someone who is not ready to change.

Among the principles in this section, the most important rule is to cause no pain and the most important practice is to look for main themes. All else derives from these two rules. Moving now from generalities into specifics, here is a step-by-step review of the palm-reading process.

Palm Reading: Step-by-Step

In general:

STOP your mind.

LOOK at the hands.

LISTEN to your intuition.

Before You Look At The Hands

Within Yourself:

Zero your mind.

Take several deep breaths.

Remember your unity with your friend.

To Your Friend:

Maintain a calm silence.

Explain briefly that lines and mounts can change, so he has control over his own life. Ask if he is right- or left-handed and how old he is.

While You Are Looking At The Hands

Within Yourself:

Keep half your attention focused in on your center and half of it focused out toward the hands.

Scan the hand. Note the relative strength of the quadrants, the temperature, sweatiness, skin texture and length of fingers, including the relative length of the three phalanges.

To Your Friend:

Maintain a calm silence.

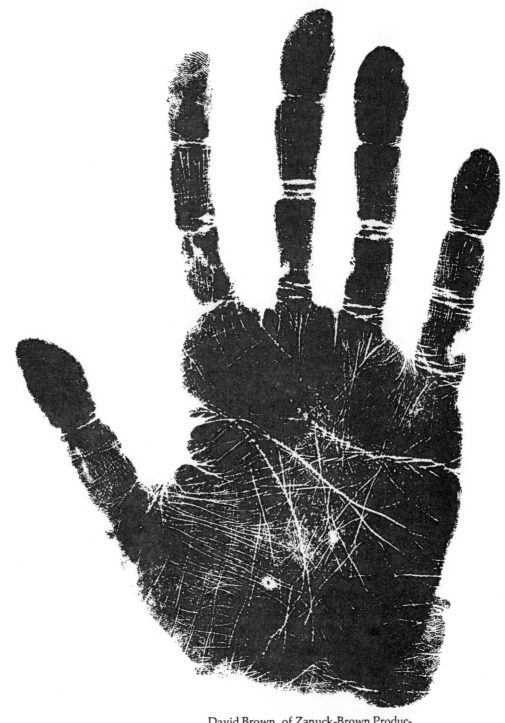

David Brown, of Zanuck-Brown Productions, is one of the most successful film producers in the entertainment world, with hits like *Jaws*, *The Sting*, and *Jaws II* to his credit.

131

Identify the basic hand type (square, long, bony, fleshy, etc.)

Turn the hand over and check the nails for signs of health.

Identify the shape of the fingertips.

If your friend gets nervous, tell him that you always look for a while before beginning to talk, so it doesn't mean there's anything wrong with his hands.

Look at the set of the fingers, noticing which are bent toward the others, which are curled up and which are rigid.

Bend each finger slowly, listening with your inner sense for the degree of flexibility or tension. Remember which fingers on both hands stand out as exceptionally rigid or tense.

Look at, perhaps run your fingers over every mount, noting the fullness or firmness of each one:

Venus
Luna
Upper Mars
Lower Mars

You still haven't said a word about the hands.

All mounts under the fingers. Note any peculiar marks on the mounts, such as stars, crosses or grids.

You're waiting until you get the whole picture before talking.

Look at the lines.

Note their clarity, depth, and where they begin and end. Look for breaks, branches, dots, bars, islands and so forth. Notice any color changes in the lines such as black, red or puffy white areas.

Examine the:

Life line
Heart line
Head line
Fate line

David Cassidy, internationally known
singer-actor.

Inner Life line
Line of Apollo
Health line
Marriage lines
Children lines

Also look for lines of influence, noticing from where they originate and to
where on the palm they are carrying
energy. If there are many extra lines
don't try to read each one; remember
that webbed lines mark a high-strung
personality.

Look for special marks:

Girdle of Venus
Ring of Solomon
Mystic Triangle
Healers' Marks

Ask yourself what the main themes of
the life are.

After you've looked at and listened to
everything, take a deep breath and let
the information come together in your
mind. Go back to the things that particularly caught your attention (tense
or flaccid fingers, broken lines, unusual marks and so forth.

After you've gathered together all this
information in your observing mind,
turn your attention to your listening
mind. Take a deep breath and let your
intuition well up inside you. If nothing
wells up, don't feel let down. As long
as you don't want it too much, it will
come.

When you have a general idea of what
you're going to say, size the person up
and decide what's the best way to express yourself to him. Be kind.

Calm silence.

Actress Janis Paige appeared on Broadway
and then on film in *The Pajama Game,*
toured nationwide with *Mame,* and has
appeared in many movies.

Continue to keep half your attention focused in on your breath and half focused out toward your friend.

Tell him what the palm told you, speaking slowly and clearly, asking if he understood you every time he gives you a blank stare.

Let your intuition guide you about where to begin. Every hand is unique, every reading takes place at a unique meeting point of time, space and mind. There's no set pattern to follow when saying aloud what the palm has silently said. One can begin with the life line, describing general vitality and life history, and then move on to the mental, emotional, vocational and marital aspects of the life as reflected in the other lines.

Sometimes it's best to begin with a description of the character as shown by the hand shape, fingertips, and tension patterns of the fingers.

Continue to breathe deeply.

Still other times a health problem or a glaring conflict will demand first attention.

As long as you touch on the meaning of all the major lines and mounts in the context of the hand and fingertips, you'll do fine.

Ask yourself:

Does he understand what I'm saying?
Do I understand what I'm saying?
Is what I'm saying appropriate to this person's life at this instant?
Listen for the answers to these questions in your heart or abdomen, not in your head.

Bob Rafelson, director of *Five Easy Pieces*
and other distinguished films.

Be sure that:

What you say is exactly what you mean.
What you mean is what the marks and energy of the palm mean.
You have opened up to your intuition and are listening to what the palm is saying.
When you've said everything you have to say, ...

Ask your friend if he has any further questions.

If the question can be answered directly from the palm, answer it as best you can. Many people ask questions like, "How many children will I have?" "How many marriages?" "Do you see a trip coming up?"

As long as you make it clear that the hands represent probabilities, not certainties, and that the person can often change his lines, answer these questions.

If the person asks about death or seems to be asking you to take responsibility for a major decision in his life, do not answer the questions directly. Questions in this category include:
"Should I marry ?"
"Should I drop out of school?"
and the old standby,
"How long will I live?"
Bear in mind that you are not a judge, a doctor or a therapist. You're a friend who's reflecting the meaning of the hand.

See below.

Postgame Wrap-Up

At this point in a reading, sit and think for a few minutes, summing up the person's general temperament and situation, and silently asking what the main themes are and what changes might be most appropriate in the person's life. Your friend might get restless, but if you keep a light touch on his hands and glance at him from time to time he'll feel reassured. Don't rush yourself. If you don't feel comfortable giving suggestions or it doesn't seem right in the situation, don't say anything. However, there are times when a person will ask for a palm reading at a time when he feels confused or trapped. If you're aware of some options for feeling better which he hadn't heard of, you can show him that more avenues are open to him than he previously thought.

Poor diet, lack of exercise, and fatigue are main causes of ill health and ragged emotions. Boredom, loneliness, anxiety, and even a feeling of being unloved can be partially alleviated by changes in diet, rest and exercise habits. Anxiety can also be chemically induced. One has to be a bit nervous to start smoking, drinking stimulants, and taking other drugs, but the physical effects often outweigh their original psychological causes. Ask, "Do you exercise? Do you eat sugar or processed food? Do you smoke? Do you take drugs? Do you drink coffee?" Anyone who answers no—yes—yes—yes—yes (or even *one* yes) deserves to feel alarmed, unhappy and irritable, since he's working hard at making himself that way.

A few simple changes in lifestyle can alter a person's mindset dramatically. Many people sit at a desk all day and go home to vegetate in front of the tube. Finally, they wonder why they don't have any energy. They're too tired to exercise. They feel heavy and useless and undersexed. And why? Because their blood is not circulating, their breath never reaches the bottom of their lungs, and consequently they feel crummy You needn't suggest that your friend go run a marathon, but you can constructively point out the clear relationship between a depressed weak body and a depressed weak mind. Even a long walk after dinner would help.

If you're familiar with various forms of diet, yoga, martial arts and meditation, cautiously suggest one of them as seems appropriate. Also, try to be aware of good doctors, psychotherapists, nutritionists, acupuncturists and other helpers in your community, since one of your most valuable functions as a palmist is referring people to experts more qualified to help with your friends' specific problems. Your suggestions should be based on a valid intuitive reading of the hand and should not be preformed in your mind just because you happen to enjoy doing a particular thing. Not everybody *likes* to jog. If your friend seems resistant to your suggestions, reflect once more to see if some other change might be more appropriate. If you still meet resistance, cheerfully end the reading. When he's ready to change, he will.

I distinguish between suggestions to do something specific, like marry a certain person or move overseas, and suggestions of some long-term activity for personal enhancement, like giving up smoking or taking up running or meditation. In the first instances, someone has several clear options and you are advising him to do one, probably to the exclusion of the others. In the second, you are making general suggestions which the person can follow to a greater or lesser extent, and which are likely to cause increased vitality and happiness. By making a few general suggestions you broaden the options available to the person while leaving the specific decisions up to him.

Palm reading—or palm listening—is a pleasant way of getting closer to other people. Whether you use it as a party game, a way to size up potential friends or business associates, or a tool for self-knowledge, you will always end up feeling your heart more open to humanity. If practiced in a spirit of humility and from a sincere desire to hear other people's stories and sympathize with them, palm reading is an endless source of pleasure and interest. You can watch your own hands change, and there are twice as many other palms to read as there are people in the world. Every hand tells its own story, yet all hands are fundamentally similar. Focusing on the hands is one of many ways to appreciate the diversity and the unity of human beings.

Your intuition plays a crucial role in developing the sympathy and insight necessary to do an appropriate and positive palm reading. If you latch onto the idea that you yourself are doing something for some lucky other person, intuitive truth will fly out the door. An accurate reading happens when the palmist combines learned information with spontaneous intuition in a spirit of humility. Study and internalize the basics and then when you look at a hand, switch to automatic pilot. It works nearly every time.

If you still doubt the power of your intuition, remember that just as your two hands give balance to your body, so the two faculties of intuition and intellect balance your mind. Use your mind and your heart, your reason and your intuition—

Use both hands!